CW01310671

The Dining Room Wall

by

Jessie Loughran Butcher

Bloomington, IN Milton Keynes, UK
authorHOUSE®

AuthorHouse™
1663 Liberty Drive, Suite 200
Bloomington, IN 47403
www.authorhouse.com
Phone: 1-800-839-8640

AuthorHouse™ UK Ltd.
500 Avebury Boulevard
Central Milton Keynes, MK9 2BE
www.authorhouse.co.uk
Phone: 08001974150

© 2007 Jessie Loughran Butcher. All rights reserved.

No part of this book may be reproduced, stored in a retrieval system, or transmitted by any means without the written permission of the author.

First published by AuthorHouse 6/19/2007

Printed in the United States of America
Bloomington, Indiana
ISBN: 978-1-4343-0765-1 (sc)
ISBN: 978-1-4343-1326-3 (hc)
This book is printed on acid-free paper.

This book is dedicated to
Rob, Gra, and Ruth

Contents

Chapter 1	Four hundred year old portrait	1
Chapter 2	Wedding of Marie Baker	5
Chapter 3	Anglo Indians	13
Chapter 4	The Railway Family	19
Chapter 5	John William Cranston	25
Chapter 6	Snooker	39
Chapter 7	Man eating tiger	53
Chapter 8	Inspector of the Police	65
Chapter 9	Call back from death	83
Chapter 10	Wynberg Allen	89
Chapter 11	Memories of the Raj	149
Chapter 12	Leprosy	165
Chapter 13	Turn of the Century	191
Chapter 14	Millennium	201
Chapter 15	Golden conclusion	215

Chapter 1
Four hundred year old portrait

A tall, handsome, middle aged man, immaculately dressed entered the stately home belonging to the Heritage. By his side walked an equally tall and eye catching middle aged woman. Both had suntanned complexions, rather more sun tanned than if there was no inherent pigmentation to begin with. They walked with aristocratic dignity, shoulders back and with strong confident footsteps.

They paid the £4. entrance fee required and were warmly welcomed by an elderly woman who asked them to sign the visitors book. The building was a magnificent piece of British architecture, constructed of grey stone with arched windows and entrance doors, it stood in the centre of a manicured lawn which was scattered about with a few large specimen trees. Around the building and framing it, to add to its air of wealth and dignity, was an ancient creeper. It was a splendid house.

There were no other visitors there at the time, so the old woman gave the couple her entire attention. The great castle doors opened into a dark entrance lobby, there were no windows to let in the spring sunshine. She closed and locked the doors behind her.

"This is my sister" said the man, "I am the eldest son of a family that has particular interest in this place". She said nothing. "She is the youngest daughter of the family". The old woman eyed the man and woman up and down, with interest..

She proceeded to lead the way into a large and richly decorated hall. Huge paintings hung from every available space on the wooden panelled walls, the ceiling looked as if it could reach to the sky. Banners and pennants hung from poles that protruded over doors.

"These pictures are all wired and alarmed" she said. "We had to sell many of them half a century ago to pay for the restoration of the building. The remaining ones are wired against burglary." The visiting couple walked in silence, gazing in awe at what might have been theirs some day. "Do you live here" asked the woman, "Are you related to the family?"

"I am the widow of the last surviving member of the family, my husband died many years ago, we never had any children. I myself am an Italian, a professional musician in my youth, we continued to live in Italy until my husband's death. The building remained in the care of the keepers and still is, although my husband made it over to the Heritage. The brother and sister listened intently.

They left the vast entrance hall and entered the library. There were many valuable pieces of porcelain amongst the huge bookshelves. Step ladders were place here and there so that one could access the upper shelves by wheeling them into place. Amela was particularly interested in the porcelain, having been a collector herself for 40 years. She expressed her interest having asked some pointed and knowledgeable questions.

"All the pieces in the house are copies of the original, they have been put here while the priceless pieces of Ming and Misen are placed in a vault for safe keeping" the old lady said. Amela told the Italian woman of her own porcelain collection which at the very best would be valued at no more than £10.000. "My pieces are all coffee cups," she said, "of most manufacturers, but I'm afraid there is no Ming or Misen amongst them"

The old lady continued, "There is only one piece of original Ming in the house", she said" Nobody but I knows which one it is"

By now, Steele had switched off this boring woman's talk and walked away to view something else in the library. Amela tried hard to see which of the pieces was original - they all looked pretty much the same to her and anybody else who cared to study them closely. They walked into another room, must obviously have been the music room. A large grand piano stood at one end, the furniture was faded and deep seated. High backed sofas, which one felt if you sat in, you could never get out of again, were interspaced with fabulously carved dining chairs.

Amela asked about the piano. "I was a professional musician in my youth", she said" Now we have musical evenings when a few of my professional musician friends, come with an instrument and we play together".

"Play something for me" Amela asked. The old lady sat at the piano and loosened her arthritic fingers by rubbing her hands together, then with super confidence and efficiency, she pounded out Beethoven's Symphony No.14. When she had finished, she dismissed the admiring comments that Amela had made and proceeded to a table covered by a runner. She removed the runner, lifted the table top and ran her fingers lovingly over the rim of a Chinese bowl that lay hidden in the hollow of the table, she said nothing, replaced the lid and the runner and lead them out of the room.

Was she trying to tell her visitor that this hidden piece was the original Ming?

The dining room was long and narrow. Spectacular curtains with golden tassels and knobs, rich in colour, framed the line of windows that overlooked the grounds. In the distance, which was barely visible above the trees, was the top of what appeared to be a ruined castle. A turret and a tower protruded above the green branches, the dense green undergrowth obscured the rest of the ruin. Steele paused and pointed to the ruin.

"What's that?" Steele asked.

"Oh that," said the old lady, "It was the original castle, some hundreds of years ago it was given to the family as a reward for some noble deed that the ancestor did for the ruler of the land. Over the centuries it fell into disrepair and this house was built in its stead, nobody ever goes there now, it is quite out of reach in distance and in time."

"Mmmmmm. Interesting" he thought

She continued to point out the salient features in the dining room to the two visitors. The long and imposing table was laid as if some illustrious visitors were expected for dinner, the glasses clearly cut by hand from the very finest crystal. The crockery was hand painted with a different scene on each piece, and probably a wedding gift from a famous and sought after porcelain manufacturer. Amela was gazing at the chandeliers, the painted ceiling and the modern electric lighting which had been installed during the twentieth century. She looked at the numerous paintings which adorned the wall, until her eyes fell on one in the far corner of the room.

It was a painting of a man in a magnificent cloak, wearing a dashing plumed hat which matched his doublet. Gold braiding and detailed ornamentation decorated the rich plush material. His face was tanned, he had dark hair and dark eyebrows, no moustache, so you could quite clearly see the detail of his eyes, nose and mouth.

Amela touched Steele's arm, quietly pointing to the painting, "Look at that", she said, "Who is that like?" He gazed in silence at the painting. They did not confer, both stood spellbound. It exactly resembled their middle brother. Every feature was identical, the expression of the eyes, the wry smile upon his lips - the narrow aristocratic nose. They continued their tour in stunned silence. The old lady said goodbye, and the brother and sister walked out into the bright spring sunshine. They had just seen a picture of their middle brother hanging on the dining room wall, amazing thing was, that picture of Alston had been painted four hundred years ago.

Chapter 2
Wedding of Marie Baker

"Queen Victoria, very good man" the Indian was overheard to say in a market place. The stall sold spices of numerous colours piled up high on a platform, a flimsy canvas like covering supported precariously on four crooked poles, constituted the roof, it was sufficient to keep out the hot sunshine, but should the monsoon rains begin in mid June as they usually did, all this exotic merchandise would be sold from inside a small shop which opened onto the busy pavement.

Scenes like this were common, the smallest villages, bustling towns or the gigantic heaving metropolis all had numerous such stalls. Calcutta boasted a population of several million. The Indians ranging from the super rich to the wretchedly poor who flocked to the city in droves. Every one was shouting. The noise was beyond description, the pushing and shoving ceaseless. Women with enormous baskets of vegetables and live chickens were seen to be weaving their way through the crowds to probably a market place somewhere in the vicinity.

A child was urinating beside the road and was narrowly missed by a passing rickshaw. The interminable bicycle bells were trying to warn pedestrians to get out of the way - but nobody listened, certainly nobody moved out of the way even if they did hear. Motorised transport had not yet arrived in Calcutta, after all, this was during the nineteenth century.

Amidst this melee of confusion the railway station of Howrah was springing up, accommodating the umpteen newly laid railway lines that were being laid across the sub-continent. Engineers, mostly from Britain, were being shipped out to mastermind the gigantic operation. The huge vault like roof was supported on iron pillars and girders that looked like they'd last a millennium. Platforms, waiting rooms, ticket offices, restaurants for the different classes and nationalities were being built to accommodate and satisfy the anticipated millions who would subsequently use such a place. Vendors of hot spicy foods, sweetmeats and garam chai plied their wares whenever, and where ever they could. Every one was shouting.

Small earthen ware drinking pots were used to serve the chai, after use they were disposed of where ever they happened to be emptied. Litter of paper and rotting vegetable lay everywhere, occasionally a bull or cow walked up to the piles of leaves and foraged for a morsel to eat. Monkeys ran along the upper parts of the building, close enough to the workmen and coolies to be touched.

Scores of women were seen to bring small bundles of chapattis and curried vegetables for their men folk. The baskets on their heads usually held a tiny baby whilst one or several others hung onto their mother as they wove their way through the crowds.

Occasionally you'd see a smartly dressed British gentleman emerge from hiding and observe the construction work. He usually swung a cane with an air of superiority and gave orders to the well dressed Indian who followed in his footsteps. It was far beneath his dignity to order the workmen himself - oh no- he'd order and command through a spokesman and heaven help anyone who disobeyed. The dust of the streets was replaced when the rains arrived, only to become mud and slush every where. The city stank of sewage. Rats scuttled in alleyways and were brazenly seen in the corners of shops and stalls.

Women wore brightly coloured saris despite the menial work they did. Men were clothed in dhotis and were more often than not, barefooted, as were their wives. A loud chugging sound was heard in the distance, people cleared the tracks, some huge rolling stock was being brought in filled to the brim with rocks and stones which had to be laid between the rails. If there was a casualty, it was not sufficient to suspend work - after all the railway network had to be completed.

Further down the road, was the British quarter. Only the rich Indians and the British could afford to live here. Separating the huge western style shops were scores of tree lined streets and fashionable apartments. Carriages and tongas were seen to carry the more illustrious inhabitants. Fashionable restaurants served tiffin, afternoon tea, gin and tonic and of course grand and beautifully presented dinners. You'd frequently see an Indian bowing and scraping and playing host to a group of immaculately dressed westerners. The women would be wearing elaborate head gear with feathers and satin hanging provocatively over their faces. The Indian host would try to emulate the air of the white man by snapping his fingers so summoning a bearer to fetch more of what ever it was the British desired.

Amongst the shops, which sold jewels and fabulous materials was an English furniture shop. The name above the entrance read B.H.SMITH & Co. The showrooms were filled with beautifully made pieces, sideboards, tables, chairs and wardrobes, Victorian by design but made in India. You'd occasionally see a well to do British couple browsing through the furniture, friends perhaps of the owner or some one who had been recommended by a previous customer.

The owner came out on several of these occasions, a tall, gaunt looking man, always dressed in a dark suit with a long jacket, possibly very handsome at some point in his life, but alas the looks had long since left. There were no rats or mice or anything like that to be seen here. The fans whirred incessantly, and there were comfortable sofas dotted around here and there for use by the prospective customers whilst they slowly made up their minds.

Rumour had it that Gerald had been seriously ill at some time, he'd employed a beautiful trained nurse to look after him. Nobody knows what the illness was, but it went on for some considerable time. Could it have been consumption, most people die of consumption - but what ever- Gerald recovered. Beulah Hope, Gerald's mother died and left the business to her only son. Gerald was a bachelor. The business continued to prosper during his illness, making vast sums of money. Had it not, he might have had to employ an Indian to take care of him, heaven forbid.

The name of the nurse was Marie Baker. A spinster about middle to late thirties in age. She had been raised in a town in the Central Province of India by an adoptive aunt. Rumour had it there were several little girls whose parents had died during the civil unrest in Russia and were adopted by a couple who had their names changed to the easily pronounceable name of Baker The girls had been raised since infancy in India, been privately educated and respected where ever they went. Marie, Evelyn-May, Cecil and Ivy looked similar and could have been sisters, Louise Amdia was a tiny scrap of a thing and might have been a cousin to the others..

They had escaped during their infancy and youth from Russia and had spent most of their lives in Jubulpur . The house they had been brought up in had an imposing drive which lead to an even more imposing mansion. It could quite easily have been the setting for a period costume drama. They lead sheltered and protected lives. Private tutors came to the house to give lessons. English was the most important subject, music ranked high on the list of "musts". Finishing school was unnecessary, as etiquette, manners, decorum and deportment were all included in their every day lessons.

The gardens were tended by an army of malis. The old Aunt never so much as entered the kitchen to lift a finger in any task that resembled menial. Dhobis came and went on a weekly basis, bringing enormous bundles of spotlessly clean linen, perfectly laundered. In return he would collect a huge pile of soiled garments.

The Dhobi book was brought out each week when he was seen cycling up the drive with this enormous white bundle almost a cubic yard in size, balancing on his head. The lady of the house would check all the items against the entry of the previous week, and then note the number of clothes and items he was taking. It was most probable that the washing was done by the side of a river- but this was never witnessed by western eyes. The iron of course was a heavy metal weapon filled with hot coals. The result was perfect laundry. If the frills on the edge of a pillowcase were not perfect, the item was discarded to be included in next weeks wash. The meagre pay would be reduced if this should happen. Items such as dresses and shirts brought on hangers were held by an outstretched hand whilst the dhobi's other hand steered his bicycle through the streets. This was special delivery and constituted another journey, another day.

Marie was class.

After she completed her education, she attended a large British Military hospital where she trained as a nurse. She took up private nursing and went where there was a shortage of classy western nurses, hence her arrival in the city of Calcutta.

She began working for Gerald, who seemed to respond admirable to her care and attention. He'd often lie in bed and admire her tiny waist, tightly corseted and wonder what she'd look like without her uniform and trappings. "How could she breathe" he thought. Her breasts rose and fell in rhythmic perfection, he could lie for hours admiring her and wish some how she would come close enough for him to pull her into the bed. Gerald never had thoughts like this before, he was a confirmed bachelor and dismissed this sort of thing from his mind. Couldn't understand it, must be the effects of the illness and the medication he was taking.

After a while Gerald decided to take a voyage to aid his recuperation. Maybe a slow boat to China or somewhere else, a leisurely calm and relaxing trip, quiet and peaceful and preferably without the noise and hubbub of Indians. Of course Marie would accompany him, but wouldn't it be perfect, if she did so as his wife. He plucked up the courage to ask for her hand in marriage. Marie was some what taken aback. Oh she knew that Gerald's looks were becoming more and more personal, and she realised too there was a certain excitement in her own breast when he looked at her in that special way. She did not expect this proposal of marriage.

Today, he was sitting in his high backed chair, he drew her to him, he held her hand and kissed it tenderly, he put both his arms around her slender waist, he could not feel the whale bone, only the rise and fall of her breasts so near to his face. Marie had given up the idea of marrying and concentrated whole heartedly on her work, until she started working for Gerald.

She thought about it for a moment, what would her aged aunt think and as for Evelyn-May who had already given birth to two children. Evelyn May was married at the tender age of 19.She could not think of them right now, Gerald pulled her onto his knee, "Marry me Marie" he whispered, "We can be so happy together, you can continue to look after me but we can share the same room and the same bed. We will be short of nothing, and with all my worldly goods I will thee endow." She smiled, "I don't want your worldly goods Gerald", she said. "That's not the reason we should be married" He hastened to say "No, no, we will be married because I have come to love you like I never thought it possible to love another human being." "I love you too" she whispered her heart pounding inside her breast.

They never had any children, Marie was past child bearing age by now, so life for them continued in secluded calm. They often attended the Church in which they were married. Sunday mornings, like most of the other English ex-pats found them walking up the drive to the grandeur and splendour of the Church of England. Beggars were not allowed to enter the Church compound, so they lined the streets leading to the entrance of the Church.

Scores of them with outstretched arms and open hands begging and pleading for a coin, however small its value. Many had no hands at all, fingers eaten away with the ravages of that abhorrent disease of leprosy, their feet also sloughed away by constant rubbing on rough surfaces, some of the beggars were maimed, some halt, some blind.

It was like running the gauntlet, that last hundred yards or so to the Church. Marie would gather her gorgeous gown closer to her so as no foul beggar could touch her beautiful clothes. Then they would enter the church and promptly forget the teachings of their God whose words meant nothing to them. "In as much as you do it unto one of these, you do it unto me."

The picture that hung on Gerald Smith's wall was their wedding photo. Marie was dressed in a gorgeous white full length gown, her waist cinched in to measure no more that 20 inches. She sat straight backed in a high backed chair, Gerald stood beside her, today he looked so handsome., despite his advancing years. They both looked serious, smiles were not permitted in formal photographs in those days, even if it was a wedding photo.

Today she was wearing her wedding dress. She had the dhurzi alter it so it looked more like a gown she could wear to Church or an official function without looking over dressed. Her pointed toed white, leather shoes were decorated with fine coloured embroidery which matched the work on her hand bag and gloves. Marie always wore gloves, they were as essential to her wardrobe as gowns and hats, so keeping the blazing sun from colouring her beautiful fair hands.

The Priest rose to his feet.

"Blessed are the poor in spirit, for theirs is the kingdom of heaven". Not many people took notice of what he was saying. What is this, the kingdom of heaven.? The only kingdom they were aware of ,was the kingdom on earth. A vast kingdom on which the sun never set. The great and mighty British Empire, where, given time, would be the kingdom on earth. It would be filled with Christian riches and ideals, it would do away with poverty and beggars and all that Indian stuff. Where every one who was any one would speak the greatest language on earth.

Victoria had died, years passed. India was preparing for her greatest royal celebration. The Durbar. The event would go down in the annuls of history as the first time British Royalty visited India. She would be recognised for what she was, a great, powerful, wonderful nation, divers perhaps in religions, castes and creeds, language and people, but united by the rich and powerful British Empire - the greatest Kingdom on earth.

Chapter 3
Anglo Indians

The Military sent armies of men to keep law and order in India, vast numbers of official hierarchy went to populate the administrative seats of government. British business men set up large money making factories. Trade with Europe flourished. Employment was cheap. The climate and demand for tea meant that tea plantations sprang up in the mountains of Assam, Darjeeling and further south in the Nilgiris.

Spices became sought after. Silk and pearls were a highly treasured and valued gift for the women of Britain whose men folk went abroad to make their fortunes They themselves remained at home. Whore houses, though not new in England or India or other parts of the world, began to thrive. Women were earning a very good living working here, giving pleasure to rich Indian men, and thousands of British and Europeans also. The difference was in India, all the whores, or as the decades swept by, the women in the sex industry, were all brown. Young girls, young women, firm breasted and obliging, cooed and wooed their clientele, stroking them with their painted hands, their full breasts and other parts of their bodies, in a desperate bid to make money.

They were not to be found plying their wares on street corners, but because of the moral standing of the Indians, they were discreetly kept behind heavy scented curtains in dimly lit rooms. If perchance the woman fell pregnant, and abortive attempts failed, she'd be dismissed and would continue her trade on the street, despised by all who saw her.

The women back home, the ladies in their grand homes in Britain, knew nothing of this, they just basked in the money being sent home to them. Their families were small, for obvious reasons, their men folk were rarely with them. Sometimes a bachelor would meet an irresistibly beautiful Indian woman who would not sleep with him or anyone else other than the man she would eventually marry. Try as he might to find pleasure and satisfaction in the arms of a promiscuous Indian beauty, he would find it difficult to forget and dismiss the object of his deeper desires, he had fallen in love with an unattainable goddess, who he had to marry.

In so doing he would lose rank amongst the high ranking British, and as for the woman, well who knows what happens to her. The progeny of such a union gave birth to a nation within a nation, and were known as Anglo Indians. An Anglo Indian by definition , is when a British man and an Indian woman have a child. It is not generally the other way about, i.e. when an Indian man and a British woman have a child.

The children of the first group formed a huge nation, the likes of who were raised in totally British style, in language, in home traditions, in religion, in apparel, in manners and customs and apart from the various shades of their complexion were totally and utterly British. They resented being called any thing other than Anglo Indians, they were not Euro Asians, half breeds and definitely not half castes. At birth they were almost always Christian by religion, unless at a later stage in their life they converted to another faith.

The caste system in India belonged to another religion, to the Hindus, and possibly to another era. Would it ever lose its rigidity, would the believers in that religion step outside of the customs? The pattern of social classes in Hinduism is called the caste system. People are born into the caste of their parents. There is no mobility across caste lines during one's lifetime. The system serves two important functions. First it assigns occupations and secondly the system separates the members by a complex system of purity. The higher up the system, the higher a level of purity they must attain. The lower, the more likely they are to transmit impurity. These purity restrictions appear most frequently in four areas, marriage, drink, food and touch.

Marriage is possible only between members of the same level. Drink and receptacles used are kept for that level of caste, food must not be eaten with a caste lower than your own, and as for touch, if a Brahman accidentally brushes against a farmer, a merchant, a trader or a craftsman, he had to undergo extensive rights of purification.

Way back in history, when the Aryans moved across India from their foothold in the North West, they conquered yet more people. To place the newly acquired groups into their society, they created a new caste. They placed the castes below the existing castes and called them the "untouchables". The untouchables were put outside the caste system, they were the outcastes. The purity regulations were such that not even the lowest caste could relate to them, they were assigned the worst occupations such as latrine cleaners, leather tanners and so on.

Underneath this scene of British rule, a silent resentment was growing amongst the Indians. Here was nation whose history goes back to the middle and dark ages of Europe, whose breathtaking architecture and customs left the rest of the world standing, who were being suppressed and made to feel inferior. Here for centuries, men were like demi gods, and women were to be revered and almost worshipped as child bearers,. and now being disregarded like outcastes in their own country.

With the British in occupation, the detailed ornamentation in their ancient temples was often hidden from the prying eyes of rulers and consequently fell into ruins. Male children had always been regarded as a gift from God, with a dignity characteristic of the Indian, and now, only those with a great deal of money were reluctantly treated with a minimum of respect by the British.

The custom of arranged marriages remained of paramount importance. Often, and particularly with the very poor people, marriages, or betrothals were arranged between two families with similar backgrounds, often whilst they were very young. The betrothed girl would return to her mother's home and remain there until the age of puberty, when she would go to her husband's home. Her main duty in her husband's home was to bear him sons, and of course to help her mother in law with house hold chores.

This custom spread across all castes. It mattered not whether you lived in a swanky apartment in Calcutta, Bombay or Delhi, or in a humble mud hut outside a dingy village in the south, a Hindu was a Hindu.

The main language of India is Hindi, although there are many, many languages as well, depending on where you live. The main language Hindi, that is until, the great British people came and taught the vast majority who came in contact with them, their own language - their own beautiful, universally used tongue. In decades to come it would be the language of the air, of business communication, of international travel, of the internet. It would be, if not the first, the second language of almost every nation under the sun.

Anglo Indians were extremely proud of their British heritage, they could be found guilty of thinking it was beneath their dignity to learn any other language but English. Anglo Indians travelled the earth, settling wherever they felt most at home, obviously in countries that spoke English as their first language, countries like America, Canada, Australia and of course Britain. It has been said that Anglo Indians inherited the qualities of both great nations. Apart from their super intelligence and their managerial ability, they were extremely good looking and possessed superior artistic qualities.

Actresses, whose beauty and talent spread across the globe, Merle Oberon, Margaret Lockwood and the famous Vivien Leigh. The writer of "Anna and the King of Siam", Anna Leonowens, Lord Liverpool Prime Minister of Britain, William Pitt, Earl of Chatham and Prime Minister of Britain. John Masters, author of the book Bwahani Junction which later was made into a famous Hollywood movie. Then there was Colonel William Lighter, Designer of the city of Adelaide, M..Kay author of the Far Pavillions. Wing Commander Gibson, leader of the Dambusters. Cliff Richard, Pop Singer. Loughran I.S. Commander of the 37th Fighter Squadron of the Indian Air Force, and finally, a musician of whom Eric Clapton once said, was the finest blues guitarist in the world, born Gerald, Cranston, Frederick, Loughran.

The British tried to keep the Anglo Indians down. They brought in English men who had been educated in the university towns of Oxford and Cambridge as employees to run the Indian Civil Service, people who climbed the ladder of success and rose to manage districts as large as the British Isles. No Anglo Indian ever attained to this position. They were never given the rank of officer in any of the armed forces. The better educated Anglo Indians were designated to the railways and police force. The Indian Railways were run by the Anglo Indians. Through the early part of the twentieth century and even to this day, if you made an outstanding success of your career, the British claimed you as their own. Surprising then that great actresses, writers and pop singers, high ranking officers in the forces were not British, but Anglo Indian.

Rich and well educated Indians were included in the officer rank of the British Services, but not so Anglo Indians. Did they pose a threat to the British? Despite this apparent and obvious discrimination, Anglo Indians succeeded in most fields, in industry, commerce, education and entertainment , but despite their successes, scores of them denied their original ancestry, calling themselves anything but Anglo Indians.

Along with POLITICAL CORRECTNESS (two words linked together in the English Language) came the description of Anglo Indians, mixed race, Eurasian, half breed, or mixed blood. British army personnel who married an Anglo Indian or Indian were no longer permitted to reside in the fort or barracks. They were forced to rent or purchase a dwelling outside army quarters, in towns or cities nearest the cantonment, but never within its boundary walls. It was only years before the second world war, were they given a small allowance to help raise their children, who were in fact Anglo Indians.

Through all this subcutaneous discrimination, the Anglo Indian remained faithful to the British, revelling in the superiority of their mother tongue, their culture, their religion, their traditions, their education and their festivals.

Chapter 4
The Railway Family

In the central place of honour, on the Dining Room Wall, hangs a large framed photograph. It is of an elderly lady with six young women standing or sitting around her. They are all dressed in day gowns that reach demurely to the ground, with jackets and stoles draped over their shoulders. They do not wear hats, their severely pulled back hair styles doing nothing for their severe expressions.

Marie, whose full name was Marie Blanche, sat to the left of her aged guardian. Cecile, who sat to the old lady's right, wore a stunning fur stole, further to the right of the picture, seated on a fairly high chair or much taller than the others, sat Evelyn May. In the line up behind the seats, stood Louise Amdia, Ivy and Katie. Little is known of those three, and they are not relative to the story.

It is thought and believed the six young girls arrived from Russia during the civil unrest, Their two sets of parents, for the girls were cousins, were killed whilst trying to leave the country and the girls were rescued and raised by the old lady. Their surname was changed from Rubeque to the more easily pronounceable name of Baker. They were brought up in a fabulous house named "Ferndale" in the central province of India , in a town called Jubulpur.

The photo had been taken at the turn of the century, between the years 1899 and 1903. It looked like a studio photo, but if you look closely, you'd see trees and shrubs in the background, suggesting the setting was a mature and tended garden. Evelyn May, who was some years younger than Marie Blanche, remained for the most part at home. During the cooler months of the year, Marie would leave her home in Calcutta and return to the home in which she had been raised, returning after the rains to her home in Calcutta and her husband Gerald.

Evelyn May rarely smiled, had this anything to do with her escape from Russia, memories of which lay deep in the shadows of her mind.? It is thought she had little pleasure in her life. The family enjoyed the company of friends who would visit Ferndale, enjoying a game of whist or a game of snooker in the games room. They would eat sumptuous meals prepared by the cook, drink alcohol free drinks served by the bearer, but it was never permitted for the young women to enter into such frivolous entertainment with the men.

There was an army of servants employed at Ferndale, attending to the creature comforts of all. Old friends would often bring young men with them to introduce them to the young women at Ferndale. The men were employed at the swanky gun carriage factory or the new railway station which seemed to be the hub of the great Indian Railway network.

As was the custom, the cooks, bearers and domestic servants, were of a different caste to the malies and dhobies who worked outside. The person who worked the fan was called the punkha walla, loosely interpreted means, Fan Man. No one was quite sure which caste category he belonged to. He'd sit alone for hours on the open veranda with his back to the house wall , with a knotted rope between his toes. Almost in semi consciousness, he would jerk the rope to make it wave the large fan that was suspended from the ceiling in the dining room, so causing a cooling breeze to provide comfort in the house guests seated around the table.

On one such occasion, an interesting young man came to dinner. He was tall, taller than Evenly May anyway, and good looking. Evelyn May was interested in him from their very first meeting, his looks, the wonderful way he spoke but most of all because he was taller than she was. So few men were taller than her, and it would have been unthinkable to marry a man shorter than one's self. A little premature to think of marriage at this stage, but at eighteen years of age and stepping out into life, it was never far from a girl's mind.

Jacob often spoke of his parents. They were so young when he was born. His mother Henrietta was just a teenager. His father worked as an Inspector in the railway. Jacob's grandfather had been born in Ireland and went to India with the Honourable East India Company. The British only took over the Honourable East India Company after the Indian Mutiny of 1857, it then became known as the British Indian Army. Jacob's grandfather held the rank of drum major, at that time a non commissioned officer, equal to the rank of Regimental Sergeant Major.

Since army personnel were not permitted to marry outside the establishment, it is quite likely that Jacob's grandmother was the daughter of another army officer. Jacob himself, like his father, worked as an inspector in the railway. His grandfather Isaac, joined the East Indian Railway after leaving the army in 1865.

Evelyn May listened with great interest to the tales of the Railway family. She found herself looking at him with admiration. She was still always demure, correct, serious and thoughtful."This girl is different" thought Jacob, "I like her".

As the months progressed, he found himself desiring her company above that of his colleagues or their sisters. He would rather visit her and communicate with her, than spend evenings at the railway club playing snooker with his chums.

There was no blazing passion, not then or later, but he soon found himself asking for her hand in marriage. They were married in 1899.

Evelyn May was just nineteen years of age. They moved into a very English part of Jubulpur. Marie and Gerald had bought a huge parcel of land in the area known as Napier Town, on which their retirement residence would be built. When Jacob and Evelyn May's bungalow had been built, they moved in and called it "Loughome."

It was a large beautiful building with gateposts that stood twenty five feet apart. The drive went into a covered port which was lined with palms and boganvillea, brilliant colours that only the tropical sun could produce. Three large stone arches at the front of the porch allowed light to stream in, while the slate roof kept out the summer sun.

Within a year or so, their first child was born, a boy who they named Albert Baker. It was customary in those days to give a boy the maiden name of his mother, Jacob was called Jacob Beatson, Beatson being the maiden name of his mother Henrietta. Their second child was born soon after, she turned out to be a wild young thing causing grief to her parents. She'd often sneak out late at night to attend parties and dances, returning in the early hours of the morning, hiding her party clothes in the hedge and climbing into bed before her parents noticed. Evelyn May knew nothing of these escapades, had she been found out, the teenager would have been hammered within an inch of her life.

Some ten years later they had two more children, causing their parent's no problems, conventional in their choice of friends and their entertainment. Rumour had it that the eldest of the Loughran girls, got involved with a bad lot in Calcutta, a gang of criminals, she married one of them much to her mother's concern. She later found out that the man was a bigamist, there was no divorce because their had been no marriage, but by this time she was with child, and she returned to Jubulpur to bring her son up with the aid of her own parents.

Albert was very talented, he was a sportsman and an athlete, above all he was a brilliant violinist with a rich deep voice, sounding like the black singer Paul Robson. His skills at wood carving and art were legendary, as was the handling of a rifle at a very early age. He swam like a fish, and got the nick name of Ship Loughran.

When Albert and his sister went to Calcutta, he got a job in the workshops of Gerald Smith, carving and making furniture for his excellent stores. His sister wasted no time in getting in with this bad lot and landing herself in trouble that hounded her all her life. The life in Calcutta was in total contrast to the quiet, sheltered lives they led in Jubulpur. Sin and degradation abounded every where. Temptation proving at times, to be beyond resistance.

Albert felt a little nervous, but could not let it show. This country boy was far too big, and handsome and talented to sit on the outside of all the carryings on. Inside he missed the security of Loughome, his shooting, he missed swimming in Marble Rocks, he missed his pals. He even missed trying to out swim that crocodile, the time when he shot a fish from the overhanging branch of a tree, then diving in to retrieve it, found a croc right beside him.

Chapter 5
John William Cranston

John William Cranston was the eldest son of a family of tea planters. Having lived in the north of Britain for the most part of his 25 years, he was shipped off to India to run the family business. It was the custom of the great British People to expect their first born son to take over the family business, the second usually had a career in the army and the third invariably donned the cloth - joined the Church that is. Subsequent sons and all daughters counted for little or nothing.

John William was on his way to India, the year was 1884. He was a dashed good looking fellow and rich to boot. When his father died, he would inherit the entire family fortune and live a life that most people dreamed about, but rarely achieved. The grand old ship had been at sea for more than three weeks - once it had crossed the Bay of Biscay and the interminably long days of sea sickness had passed, he enjoyed himself. Each day had stretched before him in relaxed luxury. He whiled away the hours with deck quoits, cards or roulette, he occasionally took a swim, but most of the time he relaxed in a deck chair watching either the porpoises leaping into the air or the lovely young English ladies parading themselves on deck.

Elizabeth was as beautiful as her sister Florence, both as fair as snowdrops and as delicate as lilies. Their hair was the lightest brown and could, on a sun-drenched afternoon be described as dark blonde. They never ventured into the blazing sun, both of them were very particular to relax in the shade or walk arm in arm along the decks beneath their parasols. They had flawless complexions, which they did not intend to lose to the rays of the sun.

John William thought of making a pass at them. Tonight was the Ship's fancy dress ball, he'd ask one of them and then the other to dance - he'd glide around the floor encircling their fairy light bodies in his arms. First Elizabeth, then Florence - he'd ask why they were on board a ship to India, and what they would be doing when they arrived at Bombay. How come they were travelling without a male relative or an elderly lady chaperon. The fancy dress ball was wonderful, the costumes defied description. Beautiful ladies looked even more beautiful, hair and wigs were worn to disguise the most familiar heads, gorgeous masks hid gorgeous painted faces until you could not recognise Elizabeth, Florence, Alice or Kitty.

"What does it matter" John William thought, "Tonight is the night for fun, and I'm going to get all the fun I can".

He woke up the next morning with a stinking headache, a heaving stomach and an empty bed. He couldn't remember much of the night before. Today the ship berthed at Bombay and he would be continuing his journey by train to the Nilgiri hill station of Ootycamund. He threw the last of his belongings into the cabin trunk and ordered tea.

"Indian or China tea? Sahab" the cabin bearer asked. "Indian tea man, Indian tea, there isn't any other" The cabin bearer raised his eyebrows and quickly went out of the room.

The journey by train was more than anything he could have expected. A thousand coolies scrambled to lift his trunks onto their heads. They shouted at each other and came near to blows before finally deciding on which head each trunk had to be carried. One little man with legs like sticks hoisted two enormous trunks onto his head, it looked as if his neck would break if his legs didn't.

John William had been told about travelling in India, but no amount of telling prepared him for this. Peddlers were carrying suspicious looking edibles in baskets on their heads, others were pouring tea into earthen ware mugs from kettles held aloft, the milky white liquid foaming into a most unsavoury looking beverage on impact.

Everyone was shouting.

John William almost fell over two men sitting crossed legged on the platform, one was shaving the other man's face. He side stepped a beggar who had no hands and feet, "A leper, my God, I thought those went out with the Bible."

John William took a rickshaw the last few miles out to the plantation. The evening sun had set, and a little chill ran through the air reminiscent of an early autumn day in England.

As he rounded the curve in the road he caught his first glimpse of the bungalow that would be his home for the next seventy years. It was white, a large imposing archway half obscured the veranda. Huge swaying fronds of brightly coloured bouganvillea covered the archway. The rickshaw walla rode as near as he could to the veranda, coming to a halt near two enormous earthen ware pots with ten foot high palm trees inside them.

Several Indian servants stood to attention to greet the new Sahab. The bearers wore smart white turbans and western style shirts and trousers, the cook was in white but wore a loin cloth and Indian style shirt. The gardener, the sweeper boy, the dhobi and every one else wore checked Indian clothes. With out exception everyone wore warm welcoming smiles.

Looking further over the tea plantation, John William could see women in gaily coloured saris bent forward over the tea bushes. They carried huge baskets on their backs which were suspended from a sling held over their heads. Their beautiful slender fingers speedily picked the fresh young leaves and tossed them over their shoulders into the baskets. It took a considerable length of time to fill a basket and many baskets to finally fill a tea chest. They did not pause to look at the welcoming party at the bungalow, their lives would continue just the way they were used to, working all the daylight hours, earning a meagre wage enabling them to put food in the mouths of their families.

Tea was in great demand these days, fetching a good price, possibly due to the fashionable custom of middle class Victorians who drank tea with their breakfast and when gossiping socially during the afternoon. John Williams entire crop was for the British market. On arrival in England fine tea blenders would package their selection and ship part of the load to the colonies. The British Empire had adopted en mass the English habit of tea drinking, the remainder was retained for home consumption.

The overseer of the plantation was a high class Hindu man called Tilak Chauhan, a finely boned man who's conscientious attitude towards his job left little for John William to worry about. He'd been there for many years and knew John William's father long before John was born. He was to be trusted entirely - in fact, John William soon began to regard Tilak as a friend rather than an employee - a member of his family - even though he was an Indian.

Often on a cool summer's evening, he would be seen driving his carriage to Tilak's house for company. Tilak's family came to expect the frequent visits of the Englishman and always made him welcome. Tilak's wife was a plump middle aged woman. - Tilak always referred to her as "Krishna's mother". Tilak never seemed to address her by name, and only ever spoke to her in public to give an order for more tea or sweet meats.

Apart from Krishna the eldest son, there were five other children. Beautiful children, all of them, three sons and two daughters and Krishna, making a total of six. The whole family were very studious and industrious. The boys usually had their noses in books, learning all they could about religion, the Empire, Queen Victoria and tea. Sometimes they were permitted to join in the conversation with John William and Tilak -other times they were sent to the rear of the house to continue their studies.

Krishna's mother and the two daughters kept very much in the background. They never spoke unless spoken to and unquestioningly obeyed every command Tilak gave them. The girls could not have been more than 12 and 14 years of age and were very conscious about their budding womanly good looks. Occasionally John William would hear them giggling in the kitchen and remark to Tilak of his good fortune in having such a delightful family.

Tilak, in true feigned Indian modesty, would dismiss them as a burden and of little use to him. "Sons, Sahab, is what all men should have. Daughters cost money and when they grow up, you have to pay dearly to get them married". "But Tilak", said John William, what would this world be like without such charming creatures as daughters, especially your two."

John William learned much of Indian customs and traditions - the undisputed head of the household was the father. Parents were never disrespected or argued with. Sons had to have a good education, this was paramount. One day their mother would select a suitable bride for them. The sole purpose of a daughter or daughter in law was to make a good wife and bare many sons.

The family had many religious figurines in their house, some had oil lights burning before them, others had gifts of sweetmeats and flowers about their necks. Prayers were often said by the whole family and when John William was there he was invited to join in. He did not, of course.

The family always seemed to be timid and humble, this made John William embarrassed, he knew he was superior, because he was English. He belonged to the British elite, but why were these people such inverted snobs. Surely it wasn't natural for them to always be so cringingly submissive and resigned to their low estate. On the one hand, Tilak spoke of the females as if they were a burden and on the other as if he revered their woman hood. He talked as if he held any dealing between a man and woman as sacred - damn it all - wasn't this a bit too much.

John William got the impression that visits to the temple were to worship a god whose sole purpose in life and after life seemed to have been to have sex with his spouse. They seemed to worship the act of sex. Their temples had carvings of couples copulating in the most ridiculous positions - and nobody but John William was in the least bit embarrassed by all this show of sexuality.

He smiled when he thought of his mother back in Britain covering the legs of the piano and chairs in an attempt at genteel modesty. Poor mother, what would she have to say if she caught sight of these brazen poses in the temple. Pushpa was the older of the daughters, she was more adventurous than her younger sister, soon forgetting her role of servitude and domesticity and venturing into the family room and offering an opinion on subjects such as education, housekeeping and the modern woman.

Sometimes John William would get fed up with this humble yet holier than thou attitude which all Indians seemed to display. They had nothing to be superior about, and nothing to offer him, yet they walked about with noses in the air although everyone knew they should be glued to the grindstone. On these occasions, he'd order his carriage to take him to the Institute where he could converse with his own kind on matters of real importance - The British Empire, male superiority and English importance.

Months slipped by. Strange that he discovered himself happier in the company of the Indian family than amongst his own country men. The superior whisky and base crude jokes failed to amuse him, in fact he felt decidedly uncomfortable in the presence of these English businessmen and British Army officers.

Oft times he would go back to his bungalow and fall onto his bed. The bearer would undo his boots and undress him before putting the mosquito net down over his tired body. Heavy hearted he'd lie awake all night counting the hours till the next evening when he'd be able to visit the family who made his loneliness bearable. So much had been written and documented about the white man co-habiting with coloureds or blacks, precious little about the coloured girl who is married to a Britisher.

Pushpa grew up in a warm and loving house hold, best described as a nest within the arms of two loving parents. She attended a day school along with her little sister Usha. The older brother Krishna,. like Tilak their father, was interested and occupied by the work they did on the plantation. Inside the love nest, were six hatchlings, nourished and cared for by their parents, nourished in mind and soul with the true values of life. Taught to love and respect family, children, parents, aunts, uncles, the extended family being of paramount importance. This was the added nourishment for her soul.

Pushpa was a deeply thoughtful girl. Each day before going to school, she would ceremoniously cleanse herself, put on a simple clean sari and plait exotic flowers into her raven black hair.

On her return from school, she'd help her mother in the kitchen, preparing plain but delicious food for her father and her brothers, ready for their return from the plantation Tilak worked on the plantation as his father had done before him. He had risen to the position of Manager and conducted the tea picking, packing and preparation for shipping with great efficiency. He adored his family, in particular the boys. The girls and their mother, whilst greatly thought of, were useful to have around, providing for their material needs in shelter, food and warmth, but remained second in his priorities.

In the corner of the dining room was a prayer area, where a picture of the Hindu God adorned the wall. Offerings of food and drink were placed before the picture. On various festival days, prayers were offered and every one revered and respected all the articles which were placed on the table.

She heard her parents discussing the need to arrange a marriage for their daughter. Pushpa had reached the age of puberty and needed a husband. Her mother had noticed the change in her body but had not spoken of it to Tilak. Indian women do not discuss these female changes and developments with anyone. They are silent about such personal matters, ignoring them as if they never took place. Pushpa always seemed delighted when Mr. Cranston visited the home. He sat and talked business with Tilak whilst enjoying a glass of Indian tea. Pushpa and her younger sister stayed in the kitchen, their father occasionally asking for more tea or sweet meats for their white guest.

Unaware of it at this time, John William found himself admiring the Indian way of life, so genuine, no artificial politeness, women were caring and subservient , so unlike the British lovelies he met on the cruise liner or back in England. In Britain, it was an accepted thing in middle class circles, to engage in extra marital relationships, and if not to the extent of copulating , certainly to flirt outrageously. Ladies clothes, whilst demurely covering the more provocative parts of the female form, were worn with an air of temptation and flaunted before male eyes.

Here, sitting in Tilaks house, it was completely different. Tilak's wife was squeezed into her choli and sari, and whilst displaying the middle part of her torso, did not, for a moment, suggest being provocative. As for the daughters, they were still children. It took a while for John William to notice their eldest daughter Pushpa was showing signs of developing into a young women. He had not noticed, till quite recently, that her choli too showed off her young breasts, however, the fancy drape of her sari covered them every time she ventured out of the house.

Pushpa was growing up. She too counted the hours each day till John William drove his carriage up to her humble home. Nobody had mentioned it to her, but she was well aware of her womanly good looks. She had huge black eyes in a soft brown skin, her raven black hair reached down to her thighs, she felt more like a woman each day.

Today she would pull her hair tightly back and make one plait, when she'd done that she would coil the plait round and round to make an impeccably neat knot at the nape of her neck. She would take the small red roses from the garden and pin them all around the knot. She'd ask her mother politely if she could borrow the fine gold ear rings she'd been given as a wedding present. Today she would put kohl on her eyes to set off the whole stunning effect.

Pushpa's heart jumped as she heard the wheels of the carriage on the drive. "How do I look Usha?" she asked her younger sister.

"You look very pretty, you look as if Papa is arranging a marriage for you and the groom's father is going to look you over."

"Don't be so silly, Usha," she said. She smoothed her blue sari with her hands and made for the family room. Pushpa's English was improving. At school she'd been learning quite well, her teacher was happy with her, but she most enjoyed the sessions she was having with Mr. Cranston.

Tilak had at first been very pleased that John William was teaching his children English. The boys were doing very well, Pushpa was doing even better. She looked forward to the classes and did the home-work John William asked them to. Sometimes Tilak felt a little troubled by the way John William looked at Pushpa. Long lingering looks which said a thousand things that no one but Pushpa could interpret. He smiled intimately at her, momentarily ignoring the boys and Usha.

He encouraged them all with spelling, grammar, pronunciation and poetry, but it soon became obvious to Tilak that Pushpa was his favourite. She tried very hard to please him, Pushpa was like that, warm, kind, vivacious and happy. She was turning out to be quite a beauty. He would soon have to find a husband for her. His savings had mounted considerably, he would be well able to pay a handsome dowry and give her a lavish wedding.

That night he'd noticed the way Pushpa had put her hair up and worn flowers round the knot at the nape of her neck. He noticed the way her young breasts filled the cholee she wore with her sari and the paint she'd put on her hands and feet. She was wearing the ear rings his own mother had given to his bride the day he got married. She looked as if she were trying to attract a husband. How had he failed to prepare for this day! Suddenly it had come upon him as a surprise. His daughter was sixteen and needed a man.

Tilak felt unwell. A little pain of indigestion weighed heavily on his chest. It had come on and off for some time now and he'd have to seriously consider taking on easier work. Walking round the plantation was getting to be too much of a strain. Tomorrow he'd ask John William if he could do more desk work, the accounts perhaps, or have the leaf samples brought to him in the office for analysis, thus enabling him to order different parts of the plantation to be picked at different times. The secret in good Nilgiri tea was to always pick the most tender young leaves before they got too big and course.

Somebody was sitting on Tilak's chest. He began to perspire heavily. Why didn't somebody take this steel band off him. The pain was excruciating. He tried to cry out. "Look after my family, Sahab".

Nobody heard him. Krishna's mother ran round frantically telling one of the boys to call John William. "Your father needs a Doctor, hurry, please hurry". Tilak died before the Doctor arrived.

A ghostly silence fell over the Indian household. John William had been told that Indians generally wail and cry aloud when a loved one dies - it was not so. The funeral took place later the same day. The body was carried by Tilak's sons to the funeral pier outside the town. Male relatives and friends all wearing white, stood around chanting prayers.

John William watched in silence as Krishna took a flaming torch and set light to the bier gazing at the flames leaping up and engulfing the body of his father. His final duty to Tilak had been performed. Krishna was now the head of the household. John William offered Krishna his condolences and his father's old job, who better than him to continue in the family tradition of Manager of this vast plantation.

Krishna refused, he said he'd be moving to Calcutta to take up teaching work and his mother and family would be accompanying him. John William tried to imagine life without Tilak and his family. What would he do with the empty hours he had previously spent in their home? The Institute left him feeling empty, he'd recently only felt fulfilled in the Indian's house. Letters from England were always welcome but infrequent. His mother would write gossipy bits of news about old friends, neighbours, romances, births and deaths. Father would only write about the family fortune.

John William decided to go back to England. He gave orders to have a trunk packed for the hold and two smaller trunks for the voyage, "Wanted on voyage" the labels read. "I'll take a holiday and put behind me this involvement with the Indian family", he thought. He missed Tilak, "Tonight I'll go and say my goodbyes."

John William wanted to cry. Men never cry , certainly not English men, he tried hard to display a stiff British upper lip. He told the coachman to wait as he walked into the little Indian home. Everything was packed up, people he recognised from the funeral were bustling about putting boxes onto bullock carts and rickshaws.

Pushpa was crying inconsolably. Usha tried to comfort her but to no avail. "Mr Cranston, Pushpa doesn't want to come to Calcutta because she is learning her lessons so well here." John William's heart stirred in his breast. If she'd been English he'd have......

She was beautiful. Her magnificent hair hung in a single plait down her back, her soft gentle hands hid her face as she pleaded to be allowed to stay at Ooty. "She can stay at the plantation," John William said to Krishna, "I'll make sure she goes to school and continue with her studies. Krishna seemed relieved by John William's suggestion. The light had returned to Pushpa's beautiful eyes.

"See" said Usha, "Mr. Cranston will look after you, He'll be like a father to you now that Papa has died. You'll have an English father" said Usha, "Pushpa, you'll be an English lady."

Pushpa could not understand the way she was feeling. She did not want Mr.Cranston to be her father, and try as she would, she did not want to be an English lady.

She felt a strange exciting feeling when he held her arm one day and stopped her whilst she carried a tray of cups into the kitchen - he'd looked into her dark brown eyes, long and lingeringly, he smiled a very weak smile, then let her arm go. She proceeded to go into the kitchen. She liked that, but Pushpa knew that it was wrong and dangerous to encourage Mr.Cranston. Nothing but pain, heart ache and sorrow would result if she accepted these looks and allowed him to hold her arm.

It would now be Krishna's job to arrange a marriage for her. As far as John William was concerned this was not an honourable way to behave. Tilak had trusted him, and the family had consented to Pushpa staying at the plantation - as his daughter. He found it increasingly impossible to look on her as his daughter. She was lovely enough to be a woman, and the look in her dark eyes suggested, perhaps, that she did not regard him as a father -but as a man.

He longed more and more to hold her in his arms, to feel her young vibrant body against him. He longed to look into her smiling eyes and touch her soft delightful brown skin. He longed to kiss her slender tapering fingers and warm parted lips. He didn't of course, nor did he speak to her of his desires. John William was twenty seven, Pushpa was sixteen. He'd so missed a woman's company and despite the eligible sisters of friends who had constantly been paraded before him, he was still alone.

He got used to having her on the plantation, he enjoyed her laughter, her funny childlike yet womanly ways. He could not help noticing her beautiful breasts or her dainty feet. She swayed in an enticing manner. John William fought the temptation to hold her in his arms. Pushpa wasn't the sort of girl to allow a man to caress her unless that man was her husband.

One day he could resist her no longer. He walked past her open bedroom door, her magnificent black hair was flowing round her body, she brushed it with long rhythmic strokes, it shone like a panther's coat. He pushed the door wide open and stepped inside, then firmly slipped the bolt behind him. He put his strong hands around her waist and lifted her onto a chair, he took the brush from her hand and began brushing her hair. It came to life in his hands, he lifted the dark tresses to his face and kissed first one handful and then another. She stood still and watched him in the mirror, then slowly she turned to face him.

"Oh Pushpa, I'm sorry," he said, "I shouldn't have done that. " She didn't say a word, just pulled his head firmly against her full breasts. John William felt as if he were drowning, the infinite sweet pleasure of her ripe young body - he had to possess her - to drink fully of the cup of pleasure forever and ever again. "Pushpa, I have to marry you," he said.

What can I say about the opposition their families would offer. John William Cranston was disinherited. He never returned to England. His proud and noble father never communicated with him again before dying of a broken heart. Nobody claimed the plantation, it now belonged to John William., that was all, every thing else had gone, he'd lost his family, his title, his mansion, estates, and several other tea plantations.

John's mother couldn't believe the news when she heard, she thought at first it was idle gossip. This was the worst thing that could have happened to her. The papers reported many mixed marriages, but God forbid it should have happened to her family.

John William married Pushpa in 1886. What a catastrophe! Queen Victoria had been on the thrown some 50 years. The Empire was going from strength to strength. Industry and mining flourished and brought great wealth to the British people scattered afar in the Colonies.

As for Pushpa, her family regarded her as dead from that day on, and never ever again so much as mentioned her name. She was thrown out of her religion. Formerly she belonged to the highest caste of the Hindu faith, she had been a Brahman. The day she married John William, she became an outcaste and remained an outcaste till the day she died. She gave up her strong family ties, her sensitive Indian culture, she'd done what Indians are forbidden to do, she married against her family's consent. She'd gone where Indian women were forbidden to go - to the home and bed of an Englishman.

They were married at St Mary's Church in Ooty. Nobody was very happy to take part in the ceremony. What ceremony? Can a Hindu be lawfully married to a Catholic? Can an Englishman be equally yoked with a Brahman? He could govern her, rule her, master her, bully her and use her, but could he ever be one flesh with her? Gradually John William noticed his friends and peers from the Institute stopped calling. Letters from England ceased to arrive, no news ever again of brothers or sisters, just one telegram years later announcing his mother's death.

Could the love of one woman be sufficient to make up for all this loss? Pushpa was for the most part supremely happy. Her upbringing had prepared her well for leaving her mother's home and making her husband happy. They were everything to each other, openly adoring each other and furnishing a nest that would be home for many children. He would often be seen lifting her onto a chair and brushing her hair. He would often caress her raven tresses and kiss her tender breasts when she turned to hold his head against her.

There were eight children. All were brought up to be good Catholics and named after Saints and John William's relatives. They had vowed to bring all their children up in the Catholic faith, Catholics promise to do so.. Pushpa knew her place. She was forbidden to worship again.

Outcastes have no place in the Hindu temple, and Hindus have no place in a Catholic Church.

Pushpa learned to conduct herself as the wife on an English gentleman. She tried hard to speak only English, she used silver cutlery and ate off fine china plates. She always sat at the table to eat or reclined as English ladies do, on the sofa. Apart from their light brown complexion, the children were entirely English. They were brought up as English gentry, spoke in the most cultured English accent, educated in a fine English convent and clad in the grandest fabric - English style. They were beautiful, intelligent, witty, demure, all of them that is, except Lizzie.

Chapter 6
Snooker

Lizzie was handsome, brilliant and anything but demure. She was born before her time, not in terms of weeks or months as in premature, but in terms of decades as in history - long, long before her time. Had she been born some fifty or sixty years later, she would have had a similar outlook as her peers, liberated and free.

She was born in the year A.D. 1900, it was always easy to calculate her age. As her siblings before and after her, she was sent to a convent for education. Her mother Pushpa had no say in her upbringing. Despite the fact her mother was an Indian, Lizzie's mother tongue was English. Most of her formative years were spent between boarding at the Convent and three months vacation at home. Little is known of her relationship with her mother, she practically never mentioned her.

Sometimes Lizzie would recall the miserable days she spent at the Convent. She hated the strict routine, unnecessary for the most part, but part and parcel of Victorian discipline. Confession and Church attendance were a must. She would go each Sunday and mumble the words which were necessary to receive absolution for her sins.

Just what she said to the Priest is hard to imagine. The girl was 14 years old, had not ventured from the plantation except to go to the boarding Convent where she'd stay behind prison like walls. She saw no boys except her four brothers during her vacation and couldn't even get her hands on mild love story books. Her hair was pulled back in an ageless fashion and secured with two dull looking ribbons tied near her ears.

She wore the ankle length navy gabardine tunic and white blouse which most self-respecting true English convent girls had to wear and boots which laced up tightly to just below the knee. She hated the boots. They were longer than all the other girls' boots and had twice as many eyes to lace into. She was always late for breakfast unless she got up a full ten minutes before the others, but how do you do that when you had no means of telling the time.

One day she threw the boots over the convent wall. "I think they've been stolen" she said to the Sister in Charge of the dormitory. Lockers were searched, girls were accused and everyone was given detention until Lizzie's boots turned up. It caused such an uproar that when they finally did turn up, Lizzie could do nothing but act alarmed. A tramp was accused of lifting the boots and Lizzie was locked in a cupboard for being so careless about her property and leaving it unguarded.

Maybe that was what she told the Priest the day she knelt quietly at the confessional. She saw his long greying beard peeping through the screen as she talked on, "Bless me Father for I have sinned., these are my sins....." She began to plait the beard through the wire mesh until she'd used up all the hair, then piously she slipped away, her sins forgiven! Lizzie never did find out how the Priest got free, maybe he had a pair of nail scissors about his person and cut his beard or perhaps the next person in the confessional alerted someone to his predicament!

She left the convent to go teacher training in Calcutta. Her adoring Papa sent money to make sure she continued to receive the finest education, one befitting such a spirited young English lady. Lizzie was about five and a half feet tall, much taller than her little mother. She had a straight aristocratic nose and a well defined jaw line. Her deep set, dark eyes were piercing for one so young. She carried herself as if she wore the crown of the late Queen Victoria upon her head and an ermine cape about her shoulders.

During her leisure hours she took to betting on the horses. Many times she was seen walking home, the mile or two from the race course, because she'd bet and lost her taxi fare home. Those days were very different from the plantation days or the cloistered existence at the Convent. "I'm addicted to gambling," she'd say, but no one could quite believe this genteel well educated English woman was telling the truth.

Calcutta stank. Along with the millions of people who had to be fed, housed and transported, there were millions of cows, goats and dogs roaming the crowded streets. Sewers were practically non-existent. Poor Indians gathered round communal taps as animals in a jungle would have gathered round a watering hole. There they performed ritualistic bathing - adeptly washing their arms, breasts and genitals whilst still remaining fully dressed. Indians are by and large, scrupulously clean, given the fact that most have very few worldly goods and millions go barefooted.

She lived with her sister Alice in a high rise block of flats. Alice was a fully trained respected Sister in charge of a hospital ward and didn't really enjoy looking after her slightly wayward rebellious sister Lizzie. One day Alice arrived home shortly before her sister who pushed her into the lounge waving her knickers in the air. "Are these yours my dear sister?" Lizzie teased, "I saw you step out of them on the pavement near the hospital."

Alice was furious and so embarrassed, she'd felt the elastic go soon after she left work and felt them slipping down her legs as she flagged down a taxi. Lizzie, who was only a few steps behind her, noticed Alice stepping swiftly out of them, pretending they did not belong to her. Now here was Lizzie waving Alice's knickers in the air and her dignity 'goodbye'.

They rarely went out together. Alice rarely went out. The Streets of Calcutta were so crowded and unsafe, and after a full day at the hospital she felt exhausted. Lizzie on the other hand did not get involved with anyone or anything that needed care or sapped her energy. She didn't sympathize with the wretched people who thronged the streets. She'd quite easily brush away little Indian children begging for money - and was rough with anyone who touched her fine clothes.

She never bought a single item of clothing or shoes from Calcutta, everything was ordered by catalogue from England. She always wore fine shoes by Bally, probably the finest shoe company in the world, based of-course, in England. Her suits were exquisitely cut and showed off her curves. Her bust was high and outstanding, some 16 or more inches larger than her tiny waist. She had delicate, perfect hands and feet, and slender, elegant shapely legs.

Lizzie had yet to meet a man who would take her fancy. She was twenty six years old and was still looking. She did not want to marry an Indian, they did nothing for her. She'd have loved to have met an Englishman, but it would appear all of them wanted white thorough bred English wives, all that was except Papa. "Why had he married an Indian?" she wondered, "I love my mother, I suppose, but she is definitely not of the same class as Papa and his children."

She decided to spend the evening at the Institute playing snooker with the men. Every one was used to seeing this handsome independent smartly dressed lady at the snooker table. Nobody would so much as make a pass at her, one or two had tried, only to be put sharply into place once and for all. She commanded respect everywhere she went. She placed her iced orange juice on the small table and surveyed the green bias in preparation to pot a ball. She was a worthy opponent for the best of players. She leant over the table, accurately positioning her cue, her arms were stretched before her - she hesitated momentarily and looked up as a man entered the room. he was a giant of a man, must have been six foot three and weighing about two hundred pounds. She noticed the dirty handkerchief tied in the four corners on his head. His face, hands and clothes were covered with soot, obviously from the boiler he'd been stoking on one of the many engines that pulled into Howrah. He was magnificently handsome she noted.

The man had many friends, railway people, British people and Anglo Indians. One of his best chums was a guy called John Masters. The best way one could describe John was as an intellectual romantic. His ability to judge, construe, analyse or condemn was second to none.

They'd talk for hours over drinks and cigarettes about the British way of life, their hopes and their dreams. They'd play the relatively newly devised game of snooker most evenings. Co-incidentally , strangely enough, the game was invented by a Colonel of the British Army in a place in central India called Jubulpur, in the year 1875. Locky's grandfathers, had all played this game, and it is most likely that the one who first arrived in India all that time ago was involved in the rules that finally became world wide, and was so popular in all the colonies.

The word "snooker" was army slang for a first year cadet. The Colonel, whose name is accredited with its invention, moved to a place in the Nilgiri Hills of South India in the year 1891. It was the wonderful, scenic hill station, called Ootycamund. Ooty was very, very British. The hills were dotted about with bungalows belonging to the numerous tea plantation owners of the age. Streets were laid out on a pattern you'd find in most middle class towns of Britain, tree lined, wide, spacious and quiet.

The British Colonel, took the now popular game to the British Club in Ooty. The rules, which had been sent to Britain, verified, checked and printed, were posted on the Dining Room Wall of the Gentlemen's club.

Amongst the members, was a middle aged man who was often seen to play the game, he was accompanied by an extremely beautiful woman, obviously not his wife. He was white, British and was addressed as "Your Lordship". The woman looked like an Anglo Indian, highly educated, cultured and with a face and figure to be envied and admired. Heard in the hush, hush whispers amongst the men, this lady was his daughter.

John Master leaned against the door of the snooker room in Calcutta and admired this gorgeous young Anglo Indian woman who was playing the game. His friend, the great Locky, walked in just then, still in his dirty railway clothes. The woman looked up, hesitated a moment, then with skill generally attributed to men, she took her shot.

"Where", John Masters wonders, "Did she learn to play like that. Locky cleaned up, had a drink with John before being introduced to the lovely lady. Lizzie's knees trembled as she felt his eyes on her - she steadied herself and prepared to complete the game. "I'll marry him one day," she thought, and swiftly pocketed the winning ball.

Their courtship was short, sharp and straight forward. Lizzie knew what she wanted even if Locky didn't. She encouraged his advances, she'd wait each day for him to come from his shift off the engines, he'd go straight to the Institute where he'd bathe, change his clothes and accept her invitation to dine. Together, they'd walk to a respectable restaurant and share their evening meal.

She told him all about the plantation, the convent, her brothers and sisters, and the various professions they had all embarked on. She talked endlessly about her highly paid job as an English teacher in a high school and of course she talked proudly about her English Papa.

He in turn, would talk about his austere mother, his brother, two sisters and his quiet, dominated father. "Mine is a railway family," he'd say, "My father continued in the tradition of his father and grandfather before him. "My grandfather was a covenanted servant to Queen Victoria, he came to India during the birth of the railway network, to drive one of the earliest trains across this newly laid branch to Calcutta.

"It is expected that all sons in our family join the railway and continue with this tradition." He leaned across the table and held her hand, despite his resolution not to get involved, he found himself making suggestions to her he half hoped would not materialize.

"When we have a son," he said, "he'll join the railway as I have done." Lizzie's heart almost stopped - "Was this a proposal of marriage?" She knew it wasn't just a lewd suggestion. She'd be so very willing to bear his sons, if he wished. If he wasn't sure, she'd help him to make up his wayward, masculine mind.

She couldn't wait for the evenings, she couldn't concentrate on teaching, gambling, snooker or anything other than her love. She longed with all her heart to be with him. She felt the world spinning, singing and going completely psychedelic when he held her in his arms. Ah -

what arms, they were sculpted by the chisel of God, bulging and rippling with each and every move.

His neck was broad and strong and carried the sound of his deep guttural voice like a golden trumpet. His hair was thick and dark, but it was his chest she loved most of all. Her heart would almost stop beating when he held her against the exquisitely hard muscles, "Let me stay here forever and die in your arms," she silently prayed to him.

Unbeknown to Locky, they had fallen hopelessly in love with one another. Calcutta suddenly became the most beautiful place in the world, not the black hole it originally felt to her. She saw no one and felt nothing but the power of this man. She lived to be with him and couldn't understand how she had changed. They walked everywhere, aware only of each other, where previously they were conscious of the admiring glances of people in the street. They failed to notice the torrential monsoon rains, enjoying only the warm sunny interludes.

"If anyone so much as looks at you my Beauty," he said, "I'll poke his eyes out with my fingers. "He was fiercely jealous of the men staring at her. Her outstanding breasts were for him alone, his to admire and adore. "No one is looking at me my love," she re-assured him, "only you." It did not matter about the age or colour of the men who set eyes on her, without exception, she was to be admired. The men soon became aware of the powerful man at her side and would avert their lecherous glances.

Alice went home to the plantation for a few days to see Papa. "When will you be back dear sister? " Lizzie taunted. She didn't really like Alice and hoped she'd not come back at all, that way she'd get to keep the flat for herself. "In a few weeks, I have some time to take off and besides I could do with a rest, I've been feeling a bit run down lately." "You should go down and see Papa yourself Lizzie, he's getting old you know, we cant just leave all the caring for Kitty to do." Kitty was the eldest sister and took on the job of caring for her ageing father.

Pushpa was never mentioned - she was so cruelly ignored. No-one, not even Papa recognised her worth. She had borne him eight children, given her entire life over to serve them, always keeping her

Indian influence and opinions to herself for fear of rejection. She had forsaken her family and religion and was generally regarded little more than a chattel by all and sundry. Even her Indian name of Pushpa had been changed to "Mary", a good English Catholic name. Every body now knew her as Mary, but in her heart, she was always "Pushpa".

In England women had only just been given the vote and news of this ridiculous carry-on with the Pankhursts and the suffragettes was met with mirth in the sub-continent. England was loosing her credibility in allowing their women an opinion in matters of politics. People had forgotten it was a woman who had ruled the Empire so successfully for more than sixty years, taking it from strength to strength. A woman's place, in particular in India, was in the home, to serve her man unquestioningly - it would always be the place for male superiority, especially British male superiority.

Pushpa hardly spoke. As her sons education progressed, so they occupied their father in long and heated discussions about politics and industry. Oft times they would banter about the superiority of the great English people, and Pushpa would hear them say:

"The English, the English, the English are best, God bless the English, to hell with the rest."

She longed to go to visit her family in Calcutta. She hadn't heard from them since she married John William - it was now well over thirty years later. Her mother would be dead, so possibly could Krishna. What of Usha? Did she marry the man of her mother's choosing or broken her heart as Pushpa had done.

Pushpa spent long hours in her room, no one saw the tears she shed. Not tears of regret at marrying John William, but regret about her religion and family and now this veiled rejection from her own Anglicised children. John William's ardour had long since cooled, it was to be expected, he was very old now, but she couldn't help noticing how he sought the company of his own people more and more. When she was at home, and not dwelling on her forgotten youth, she would be in the kitchen, dressed in a dull looking sari, cooking and waiting on the needs of the family. It was only when she went with John William to Church, would she be seen in a western dress.

She first noticed the hurtful remarks after the 5th child was born - "He's so much darker that the others," someone said, "more like his Indian mother than his English Papa." John William did not come to the child's defence, nor say a word about "colour not being important."

Pushpa began to realize it was important - brown skin is Indian and try as she may she couldn't change the colour. She absolutely never went out in the sun uncovered. Consequently she developed a pallid, sallow look which was not in the least bit attractive. The colour of the children ranged from the lightest summer tan to a deep rich brown - Papa's favourites followed exactly the same pattern. The lighter complexioned children were quite obviously his favourites - nobody actually put this into words because it was not recognised until many years later.

One day Pushpa could bear it no longer. She decided to put a few things into a box and go to Calcutta. She would stay in a hotel and try and find the remnants of her family. She confided in Papa who despite his Victorian values and English attitude still dearly loved Pushpa. He didn't realize how much until she left the plantation for the very first time.

His life had arrogantly revolved around himself, he hardly recognised it was she who stood by his side. He realised a little of the pain she must have felt by losing her family, he himself had lost all for her sake, but had successfully surrounded himself with a close knit family of sons and daughters. He secretly blamed her for making him forsake his upbringing and his country for her. It rarely dawned on him that the children who he was so proud of were her children also.

She hadn't the faintest idea of how she'd attempt this impossible task of finding her family. All she had to go on was a piece of paper with an address scribbled on it, it was the place Krishna and the others had moved to after Tilak's death long, long ago. The spirited young girl they'd left behind was a far cry from the tiny middle aged women who's sad countenance could not hide her crushed spirit.

In any case, if things did not work out in Calcutta, she'd go and visit Alice and keep house for her for a while. She took Alice's address from a letter that Papa had received a few weeks earlier. Alice wouldn't mind so much, Pushpa could cook and clean for her and be like her ayah.

Her search was quite hopeless - nobody remembered her family - people in Calcutta move frequently, going wherever there is a living to be made and living where ever the roof was sound enough to keep off the monsoon rains. Life was awful if you were a poor Indian who had no English contacts. INDIAN was okay if you were rich, ENGLISH was okay if you were rich or poor, although there were no poor English in India.

Pushpa had too much English in her to be accepted into Indian culture, and too much Indian in her to have any dealings with the English outside the plantation and sheltering wing of John William.

She had been in Calcutta for nine days - walking endlessly in a fruitless search, never once having seen anyone who might have been the least bit helpful. Her legs and body ached, she felt exhausted and desperate. What is despair? Do you know? People who are desperate are rarely aware of their state. Did she imagine it or was it real - some one whom she knew. She hastened her footsteps to catch up with the beautiful young woman who held onto the arm of a big handsome man.

"That is my Lizzie", she thought, "I'm so happy." She didn't call out lest she was wrong, she hadn't seen Lizzie since she had come to Calcutta more than six years before to train to be an English teacher. Lizzie hadn't written to her, to Papa yes, only occasionally, but not to her - she was so busy and so beautiful, and she looked so very, very English.

She kept her eye on the tall man till she caught up with them, weaving her way through the crowds. She took two or three quick steps to stand facing her daughter.

"Hello darling," Pushpa said to Lizzie, smiling expectantly. Oh God - Oh God, could this incident ever really have happened. Lizzie went pale and clung tightly onto the arm of her English man. There was only a moment's hesitation as recognition dawned. Lizzie then put her hand on the woman's arm and pushed her out of the way and walked straight on.

Locky did not know her heart was breaking, nor did he ever, ever know the tragic face of that woman belonged to Lizzie's mother. What had the English attitude done to the basic values of life? For the love of a man she had denied knowledge of her own mother. She tried to tell herself the action had been necessary, it was indeed not her mother. Her mother would be on the plantation with Papa, where she belonged. She tried hard to convince herself that the old lady had been mistaken -she'd mistaken her for someone else and would soon forget the incident. Locky wouldn't want anything to do with her if he knew her mother was an Indian.

Lizzie returned to the flat with Locky, trying hard to put the matter out of her mind. No sooner had the door closed behind them when she was in his powerful arms. "Tomorrow I'm going to get a special licence for us to get married" she said. They were burning up for each other. It was only six weeks since they had met across the snooker table and each day had seen them fall more and more in love. Their kisses and embraces were fast becoming out of hand and very soon they would be unable to control their wild, passionate longing for each other.

Three long agonising days later, she washed the only decent shirt he had with him in Calcutta, she bought herself a wedding ring and prepared to go with him to the Church, where they had previously seen the priest and set the date for their nuptial. Alice had returned from Ooty, and stood as their witness. Lizzie had no problem finding something stunning to wear. Her wardrobe was full of beautiful clothes and shoes, she chose a cream silk suit with embroidery on the lapels, the special finishing touch was an expensive, exotic bouquet of orchids - and she was ready.

No photographs were taken of that wedding. No knowledge of where they spent that all consuming honeymoon. It didn't really matter. What if they had flown high over the Roof of the World, or taken a slow boat to China, or spent their time together in the waiting room at Howrah Station ? It would not have mattered at all - nothing could have altered their sublime and total happiness with each other.

Time after time, day after day, night after night they tried to satisfy their passionate longing, would they ever be able to ? Would they ever want to? Could they ever stop wanting each other as they did now?

That first year passed in a cloudy haze of happiness. It seemed no time at all before they proudly stood in front of the Priest with a tiny babe in their arms. "He's so strong and powerful" said the adoring father as he looked in wonder at the tiny scrap of helpless baby he held out to the Priest, I would like to name him Iron Steel.

The Priest stood back aghast. "I'm sorry," he said, "I cannot christen this child Iron Steel, there is no such name in the Bible or among the Saints. Locky was annoyed to say the least. He had every intention of having his son christened Iron Steel. This baby was going to be harder and stronger than his father and Iron Steel were the prophetic names he had chosen - prophetic and original.

"I'm sorry", the Priest was adamant. "I can christen him Ian Steele if you like, that is the nearest you are going to get to your Iron Steel." Locky reluctantly agreed. The service complete, Locky immediately began to call him "Steele."

That night he took Lizzie in his powerful arms, "He's such a beautiful baby, Lock, we're going to have many more like him." Their happiness was complete. She called him "Locky", he called her "Lock". "He was the key," he said, "that opened the lock of her heart."

Lizzie was asleep when Baby Steele started crying. Locky picked up the tiny scrap in his arms and walked out onto the balcony. Calcutta was throbbing in the streets below, he put his mouth near the tiny head and began humming a plaintive lullaby:

> "I want you to be, little pal,
> What your daddy couldn't be, little pal,
> I want you to laugh and to sing and to play,
> To look after Mother, while daddy is away.
> I'll pray day and night, little pal,
> That you'll turn out right, little pal,
> And someday, should you be, on a new daddy's knee,
> Don't forget about me, little pal."

No one but Steele could hear the words and he didn't understand what his father sang.

Lizzie gave up her job as high school Teacher. Her life revolved around Locky, the baby and the running of the home. She was completely unprepared for the city mode of living. On the plantation, the servants saw to everything. Here she had to organise meals and shopping. She employed an ayah whose work included nappy washing, and a twenty four hour vigil of the precious babe.

Lizzie's days were spent feeding and playing with Steele when he was awake, and waiting anxiously for Locky's home-coming each day. A year passed and another baby arrived. This time it was a little girl. Locky tried to hide his disappointment. Victorian tradition, carried over into the Edwardian age, placed a great deal of importance on having male children, sons were of paramount importance, girls tended to be a nuisance, and were really only the concern of their mother. He talked little to the children. Lizzie noticed how he almost never played with Ruth May whilst he fussed over and teased Steele often and for long periods. She adored the children and longed to show them to his family. She tried to be a dutiful wife but in a very different way to Pushpa. Pushpa never seemed to forget her air of servitude, or her submissive manner. Lizzie never acquired one.

Chapter 7
Man eating tiger

It is the beginning of the 20th century. It was a popular pass time for the rich and famous, for royalty, the aristocracy of all nations to visit India, making an organised TIGER SHOOT the high light of their adventure. Shoots were organised to take place off the backs of elephants, firstly because of the unrivalled vantage point and secondly, because of the safety of the rich hunters.

It often continued for days. Everyone was kitted out in fashionable hunting costumes, finely tailored and colour co-ordinated . Topees were worn to keep out the heat, and rifles were manufactured or hand crafted for each individual. Absolutely no expense was spared. The sight, colour and drama of such an event was unparalleled anywhere in the world. Bearers and attendants were relied upon to provide comfort and refreshment for the hunters, mostly the great white hunters. Maharajahs and other wealthy Indians often accompanied the British on these "Tiger Shoots".

After each successful event, the "KILL" was laid out in front of the "Hunters" and photographs were ceremoniously taken. The animals were then taken to the taxidermist and the finished results hung on the walls of Trophy rooms around the globe. Tigers were being shot by the thousand, no thought at all being given to the fact they were fast becoming extinct. Tigers were revered by the Hindus, being a vehicle of one of their deity.

Often tigers would be wounded and escape into the jungle, to die later. Some survived by resorting to kill the slowest prey they could find, which were humans. Unlike venison , which was deer's meat, tiger meat was not eaten. Tiger fat was rendered down, and used as embrocation, the remaining part of the animal was devoured by the overhead, ever circling vultures.

In the opinion of the writer, the tiger is the most beautiful animal on earth. Towards the middle of the twentieth century, the public attitude towards tiger shoots began to change. The camera was slowly taking the place of the rifle, and organised shoots from the backs of elephants was history. India was fighting for independence, the British were no longer looked up to and Anglo Indians were often looked down upon, being the progeny of two nations. The Hindu woman who married a Brit, was the lowest of the low, often disowned by her own and her husbands relations.

By now Locky had left the railway and joined the police. Lizzie had not as yet met his family. Look at the picture of Lizzie on the Dining Room Wall. She is dignified and very beautiful, her head held erect and a half smile playing about her lips. By, her side, but in another frame, resplendent in police uniform, is a picture of Locky. He sits in a manner that exudes authority and power, his left hand resting lightly on a topee which is placed upon his knee.

Steele was three, Ruth May about two. Locky decided to take his beautiful Catholic wife to visit his parents in Central India. Evelyn May was a deeply religious woman, a non- conformist Christian who had a genuine faith in God the Father, Jesus the Son and the Holy Spirit. Locky, whilst believing from afar , was not a bit like his mother.

The old lady attended Church twice on Sundays, and several times during the week to prayer meetings and Bible studies. She genuinely believed the Bible, her faith prompting her to study the good book and learn more about its author. She lived her life as if God was in the world around her. Jacob said little, an introvert man who barely spoke but was often found to be deep in thought. Locky was in awe of his mother. She was a statuesque woman who rarely smiled and disapproved of everything but prayer.

Every afternoon, at three o'clock all members of the family and visiting guests were called to prayer. The gathering took the order of extensive Bible reading and then kneeling on the marble floor where everyone present was required to prayer aloud to God. The gathering generally lasted for an hour or so, and nobody could rise from their knees until Evelyn May said so.

Lizzie had arrived from Calcutta that morning. Locky affected the introductions. The old lady eyed Lizzie up and down, rather disapproving inwardly of her worldly, fashionable clothes and the tight way she'd belted in her waist, making her large breasts protrude in a most unladylike manner.

She patted Steele on his head. Ruth May clung to her mother's skirt, afraid of this frightening looking woman who was her grandmother. "Give her to the ayah" Evelyn May said, "We're going to have our prayer time now". Ruth May rested her curly head on her mother's breast. "It's alright Mama" Lizzie said, "She's very tired, I think she'll be asleep before too long."

The Holy Book was opened and a passage was read from the Gospels, after which Lizzie placed Ruth May in a chair with cushions around her to allow her to go to sleep. She then bent her young and beautiful knees in prayer. She thought about the confessional in Church in Ooty. She remembered plaiting the priest's beard and then having her sins absolved. It was nothing like this, how was she to approach God in this family parlour.

There was silence in the room. Lizzie had not heard a word of Aunt Louise Amdia's prayer. It had gone on for so long, a catalogue of names, of requests, of praises to Jesus Christ. She heard someone snore, it was Locky. He had been awake all night during the train journey, he really ought to have been allowed to rest this afternoon. Nobody took any notice of this indiscretion.

"Lizzie", the old lady was heard to whisper. Lizzie looked up raising her bowed head. "Lizzie, you pray now", Lizzie felt sick with nerves. She was not used to this type of gathering, she was not used to people speaking to God as if He were in the room with them. She felt like fleeing from the room. "Don't worry, Lizzie, just say what you want to, don't be afraid".

"Hail Mary, full of grace, the Lord is with Thee, blessed art thou amongst women and blessed is the fruit of thy womb, Jesus", she hastened through her prayer, "Amen", she ended breathlessly and to her surprise every one else in the room said "Amen".

How odd! How Strange! How abnormally normal. " What sort of a family have I married into, why hadn't Locky warned me ?" her mind was racing.

Her mother in law started praying. This time Lizzie did take notice. Her prayer was laced with praise and intercession, of love and caring gratitude and faith. "How very interesting " Lizzie thought, and almost meant the "Amen" she said at the conclusion of the fifteen minute prayer.

The clock struck four, the blessed hour had come to an end and not a moment too soon. She stood up and lifted her frock ever so slightly to see what damage the hour long contact with the marble had done to her knees. She rubbed them quickly. She was aware of the warm approval of this prayerful group. She smiled her pleasure back to the old lady, who only nodded.

Lizzie lifted the baby off the chair where she had fallen asleep and gave her to the ayah to look after her, then she took Steele by the hand and walked out into the brilliant sunshine. Lizzie did not mention her feelings to Locky, sensing he was as confused as she was. "I wonder what any one would say if they knew my father was a Catholic and , horror of horrors, my mother was a Hindu. She felt more than a pang of guilt as she remembered the day she pushed that old Indian woman out of her way and in so doing, denied knowledge of her own mother.

The evening meal was served by Kissen. The Indian servant woman had set the table with the barest of cutlery, a glass and a plain undecorated large white plate sat in front of each chair. The meal consisted of boiled rice, dhal with a minimum of spices, and a small serving dish of curried meat. Lizzie couldn't help but notice the way the curry was made with small pieces of meat and lots of chopped up potatoes to bulk it out and make the dish go further.

Lizzie's mother in law, whom she reverently called "Mama", served each one in turn. She walked round the table prodding the little ones if they hesitated between mouthfuls. No water had to be drunk until your place was clear, and if you absolutely could not eat it all, you were gently told "Don't worry dear, you can have it for your breakfast tomorrow."

Locky of course, knew the routine, and Lizzie soon realized you wouldn't see a grain of rice on his plate when he politely placed his spoon and fork together. Steele was too afraid to cry and even little Ruth May choked down her dhal and rice without complaining, her frightened little eyes glancing sideways at Mama.

When every plate was clear, Mama said grace yet again, "For what we have received, may the Lord make us truly thankful, Amen" Every one rose from the table. Kissen cleared the dishes away and disappeared into the kitchen. Lizzie longed to be alone with Locky, but alas, this was not to be till bed time.

Locky and his young brother were going shooting,. They hadn't seen each other for years and although Locky was some ten years older than his brother, they were close and had much to talk about. His young brother was completely in awe of him. It appeared every thing that Locky did from cabinet making to big game hunting, held the younger man spell bound. He wanted to be like him, strong, powerful and good looking with a voice that sounded like thunder and a wife as beautiful as a queen. Most of all, he wanted to be free from his mother's authority and do his own thing.

"I will be going to Church this evening," Mama said to Lizzie one day "Why don't you come with me? The ayah can look after the children". "I can't do that ", said Lizzie, "I'm a Catholic Mama". "God is no respecter of persons" her mother in law replied. So much for her excuse, she had to go. The tonga came to take them to Church. A tonga is a small carriage drawn by a single horse. The Church was a little building standing alone in its own compound, a sparse garden surrounded it. The word "Pentecostal" was painted above the entrance. Lizzie had no idea what this meant. This Church was altogether different from what she had been used to. Where were the stations of the cross, the vaulted ceilings, the stained glass windows. This Church had no platform, no lectern, no statues, just rows of wooden chairs and a piano. Hymn books were laid out and the two dozen or so church goers practically filled the room. She watched her mother in law and copied everything she did. She didn't see anyone genuflecting, there was no perpetual light to genuflect to.

The singing started and people seemed genuinely to enter into it. The Bible was read with such warmth and feeling. Lizzie was amazed at the belief and faith of the people. Her mother in law had told her there had been a revival at the turn of the century, she had been present at the out pouring of the Holy Spirit which happened simultaneously in Sweden, United States and India.

Lizzie did not want to show her ignorance, so said nothing. As the service continued, Lizzie found herself in deep concentration. She started to pray silently, something she had never done before. She found herself worshipping and praising God from the depth of her heart. Then she began praying in another language.

She didn't question what she was doing. Nobody around her questioned it either. She began to sing and sing in this other language, then without prompting, she started to sing in English. She sang for ages, praises and yet more praises to God, praises for sending his wonderful son into the world. After what seemed like only a moment, she got up with the other members of the congregation. The service had ended. She had been in prayer and praise for over two hours.

"Did you know what you were saying Lizzie?" the old lady asked her. "No" said Lizzie, " I have no idea, I only know that every part of my soul is crying the name of Jesus."

"You were singing straight from the psalms", her mother in law said. "When did you learn them."

"I don't know any of them , I only know they come from the Bible, but other than that, I don't know anything about them."

Lizzie had been converted, converted from a non-committed nominal Christian, to one that is born again. She lived now for Christ, she loved Him for all that he had done for her. Yes truly, He was the first in her life, and remained so till the day she died. Her faith was like a shield, no one could make her falter. Family prayer became the norm for her life. Locky would read the scriptures each time they gathered, but it was Lizzie who prayed and worshipped and brought the children up in the knowledge of God.

Locky was Chief Inspector in the Central Province of India., as such he was responsible for a town and its surrounding territory and masses. It has been said, he would ride his motor bike through the town with a whip in his hand, lashing out at people who might have a reputation of being homo sexual. Locky was definitely an autocratic racist.

Every village around the town of which he was Chief Inspector knew him as Burra Sahab. Sahab because he was the master, and burra because he was big and important.

One day word came to him of an incident that had taken place in a nearby village. An Indian peasant woman had ventured deep into the jungle to gather fire wood in preparation to cook the meagre family meal she would place before her family.

She failed to return for hours which gave rise to concern amongst the villagers. They went into the jungle in search of her. They took lanterns and torches and kept calling her name aloud. The only response they received was the screeching of monkeys and the hooting of owls and other night wild life. The villagers continued to search in all directions, fanning out from the village. Suddenly, there was a cry from one area, a small piece of material was found hanging in shreds from a thorn bush. The villagers gathered around to examine the find, only to be told by the husband that it was indeed a remnant of her clothes. They continued to search, finding other parts of the garments. They disturbed a pack of hyena which growled, snarled and ran away while they examined the article they were scavenging over. To the horror of the villagers, it was parts of the woman. The husband and the near relatives were devastated, they had to carry this news back to her children. Panic struck into their hearts. If this had happened once in this part of the jungle, it was sure to happen again.

They immediately got this news back to the police Sahab. Locky was an expert shot. He had been commissioned by the government on many occasions to track down and kill the tigers who had been invading the villagers and killing the inhabitants. He never failed to get the beast. He was so confident, that on one occasion Lizzie remembers him asking if he could set Steele as bait. "Don't worry Lock", he said, "I'll bring him safely back". Lizzie was incensed . What sort of a man was this, who would use his own son as bait.?

He organised about forty villagers to be "beaters" on this shoot. Each was armed with a huge wooden pole with which to thrash at the undergrowth of the jungle. The beaters would start by forming a long straight line and together would beat their way deeper and deeper into the jungle. They shouted louder and louder, all the time beating the ground before them. They slowly progressed through the jungle towards the area where the Burra Sahab was waiting.

Seated high in a tree, on a platform made from branches and tied together by rope was a "machan". Locky anticipated the animal would slowly growl its way towards him in the opposite direction from the beaters. He sat motionless. The odd twig snapped when a monkey leapt through the branches. He could hear the screeching call of a peacock. Now in the distance, and only very faintly, he could hear the beaters. As they approached, the noise became a little louder. He could not hear the growl of the man eater. Was it in the path of the beaters?

Dusk was falling. This was the expected time for the tiger to hunt for its food. The noise of the beaters became louder. The bleating of the terrified kid goat that was tied up as bait was getting louder and louder, thus luring the tiger toward it. Locky shone his powerful shooting torch around. Night falls very suddenly in the tropics. No dusk, one minute it is daylight, the next it is dark.

He could now hear the growl of the tiger. The animal was afraid. The growl turned into a roar. The beaters were approaching. They too were afraid. Locky had to be very careful where he took aim. Turning his gaze in the direction of the tiger's roar, he shone his torch. The light picked out the eyes of the animal. The tiger was mesmerized by the beam and stood still. A snarl. A growl. Monkeys and peafowl were screeching all round, warning their breed of imminent danger. A wild boar and piglets ran out of hearing, terrified of the approaching big cat.

Locky sat motionless while he took aim downward. The animal fell to the ground - dead. It had been hit right between the eyes from a distance of a hundred feet or so. The joy of the beaters is hard to describe. A bullock cart was hurriedly brought to the spot to collect the huge beast. Before loading it onto the cart, scores of villagers came to pay their last respects. Touching first the dead animal, then touching their foreheads in respect.

The unharmed kid goat was allowed to return to its poor village owner. The skin of the beast was removed with the head left on and in tact. The body left for the scavenging vultures. The skin was then packed up and sent to a taxidermist in the South of India, where it would be cured, the head stuffed and mounted, the eyes wide open., the roaring mouth revealing two rows of dangerous looking teeth.

Hanging on the dining room wall, in all its splendour is the skin of the tiger, stretching from its mounted head to the tip of its outstretched tail - some twelve or fourteen feet in length.

Hanging on the opposite wall of the dinning room hangs a large photograph of a man resting the butt of his gun on a tiger's head as it lies dead beside him. The photograph is of Locky.

Every morning, Locky would examine the tiger skin and head, counting first each of its claws, and the whiskers around its mouth. He thought the servants would rob parts of the huge animal, which was regarded as an aphrodisiac, and sell the parts in the town. He also knew that they revered the animal and longed to possess part of its sacred carcass. His life in the Police Force ran as smoothly as he would let it. He was a larger than life character, and he was a bully. His time was spent between his duty as an Inspector of Police and a "Shakari", a hunter. He was amassing skins of tigers, panthas and antelopes by the dozen, most were folded up and kept in tin trunks. The antlers were hung up as hat hooks or thrown onto the terraces to dry off in the baking summer sun.

When Steele grew older he was told to take the dozen or so tiger skins to Calcutta and sell them. There was a growing market of collectors and exporters, many of who dealt with the Americans. The skins fetched a very good price. Locky had no need of them himself. Lizzie was going through the change of life. She was forty two years of age and had kept her stunning figure since she was in her early twenties. Although she had seven children, she managed to regain her tiny waist measurements. However after the birth of her seventh child she found it more difficult to do so.

Amela was four years of age and still suckling. She was not a bit like the three sisters before her. They were delicate little creatures with fine features, small hands and feet and the makings of finely boned little women. The boys, all three of them, were bright and mischievous. Each had an ayah whose sole job in life was to tend the child they were employed to look after, until they were ready to go to boarding school.

The big, fat Indian ayah who was employed to tend the energetic hyperactive four year old was called "Bhaise". It means "Buffalo" She sat around all day with one eye on the child. Sometimes she'd find her hiding in a tree, or at the back of a pile of old furniture or behind shrubs in the garden. Bhaise could not keep up with her. One day Locky caught Amela sucking Bhaise's fingers and nodding off to sleep. This struck Locky as an uncharacteristic thing to be doing, he pulled the ayah's fingers out of the child's mouth, only to find opium under her finger nails. Locky hit the ayah hard enough to send her flying. She was instantly dismissed.

Lizzie felt unwell. There must be something she could take to stop her feeling sick. She felt bloated all the time. The five older children had gone off to boarding school in the Himalayas. After their departure each

March, Lizzie would sit around and mope. She cried for weeks on end and showed precious little interest in the home.

Wynberg Allen was one of the finest schools in the country, chosen for its high academic achievements and its spectacular setting. It was seven thousand feet up in the foothills of the Himalayas, over looking the Ganges River as it wound its way beyond the Doon Valley. In the town of Mussoorie, was a number of fine schools founded by the British towards the latter part of the nineteenth century, Wynberg Allen was one of these.

"Mrs. Loughran, you are seven months pregnant" said the Doctor. "I can't be, I'm going through the change of life" she replied . A baby boy was born two months later, a gorgeous baby boy with wavy dark hair and the face of an angel.

They named him Gerald, Cranston, Frederick, Loughran.

Lizzie had been heard to say, "I am ready to give him every thing I am."

And even though she had been married to him for fifteen years, he still had the power to make her weak in the knees and totally submissive in her body.

Chapter 8
Inspector of the Police

Lizzie Loughran was at last going to visit her father in the Nilgiris. John William Cranston opened the package that contained the photo taken on his 90th birthday, It had just been delivered by the Indian delivery walla. He studied it for a moment, then instructed the orderly to pay the man and hang the framed picture on the dining room wall. The picture was in black and white, tinted to give the appearance of having been taken in colour. The stately elder citizen sits resplendent in top hat and tails leaning lord-like upon his cane, his legs crossed in a dignified manner. Looking at the solitary picture triggered off a multitude of memories, what was or what might have been.

The year was nineteen forty six, his adult life had been so different from his youth. His wife, had died many years before, he tended to forget her real name was Pushpa, but when they were married, it was necessary for the Church records that her name be changed. He so wanted her to be British. From that day he began to call her Mary . She was known by her new name for the remainder of her life. There were no pictures of her anywhere in the house. They'd had eight children, all married and removed to other parts of the country if not to other parts of the world. Occasionally Kitty and George would come and visit, sometimes accompanied by their adult off- spring.

John William lost count as to how many descendants he had. Florence, who had married an English banker, lived for the most part in Calcutta. Her husband, had broken company rules when he married a girl born in India from an Indian mother. He had to keep her under wraps until the banker retired and was able to return to England, where he could live an open life with his glamorous wife and their little daughter. Their daughter was a joy to their lives, spreading joy where ever and to whom so ever she met. They called her Felicity.

Very often, whilst she was in India, Florence would visit and stay for months on end at Lizzie's home in the Central Province .Lizzie had settled there after marrying into the Railway family, and whose husband now was as Inspector in the Police force.

Hanging on the dinning room wall, which was almost invisible to John William's eyes, was another picture. It was a picture of a large family. His family, he didn't notice until it was pointed out to him that week, that every one was brown except him. All the children, their children's children were dark, and darkest of all was Mary. He had forgotten about her colour, failed to notice it, she had been gone for so long a time. In his heart of hearts, and in his quiet moments , which were so many, he missed her.

It was rare for Lizzie to visit, rare to even hear from her by letter. The distance of her home was well in access of one thousand miles from Ooty, and despite the fact that Lizzie could obtain concessional tickets on the railway, she never used them to visit her father.

John William knew nothing about the man that Lizzie had married. He only knew that when she was teaching in the railway school in Calcutta, that she'd met and married him within a matter of a few short weeks. This year was going to be different. John William was waiting anxiously, for in the next few days Lizzie was coming to see him, bringing with her, her two sons, the eldest and the youngest.

John William's home was a spacious bungalow set on the slopes of the Nilgiri Hills in the South of India. Around his home were scatted bungalows of lesser and greater distinction. Grand entrances to some which were discreetly hidden behind huge hedges of rhododendrons and eucalyptus trees, others less ostentatious but never the less, most desirable residences.

He could see in the distance the tea plantation that had once belonged to him and his family. He had come from Britain to manage it, part of a famous family of tea plantation owners. He did not do so for long, circumstances forced him to chose between his former life in Britain or to live forever in India.

He remembered his home in the north , a beautiful stately old place set in manicured gardens with lawns which were a vivid green all through the year. He could still see the imposing arched entrance doors, leading to a dark inner portico. He could see almost as if it were yesterday, the wide sweeping stair case lined with dozens of paintings that led to the bed chambers. What was he left with?

His mother, his brothers, his children, his grandchildren, his aristocratic friends, his country - all gone. Gone - but never forgotten.

Old men don't cry. John William was sad. Tears slipped down his lined and tired face.

There was huge unrest in the country, seemed to be worsening as the years went by. The second world war was over, a large army of Indian soldiers fought bravely in Europe and were decorated and buried there. The Cranston household was not affected by this. Certain day to day items were still being rationed, sugar and cotton being just two, but there was a super abundance of most other things, and in an case rationed good were easily available on the black market, to those who had money to buy them.

He wiped the tears from his face. She will be here in the next day or two, with Steele who was about eighteen years of age and Gerry who was no more than about three. John William had not seen any of her other children, it was almost as if she kept them from him, and the home he used to share with her mother Mary.

The old man went to the veranda as he heard the rickshaw pull up . He was overjoyed to embrace the woman whom he had not seen for over twenty years. When he saw her, he realized she hadn't changed much form the spirited young thing who used to amaze him with her modern ideas. She had the features of her mother. Her eldest son Steele helped the little one out of the rickshaw. He shook hands with his grand father and then lifted the little one up and told him to say "Hello" to the old man.

Lizzie went on into the bungalow . She vaguely remembered the positioning of the furniture and the drapes that covered the windows. Her sister Kitty came up and hugged her. Kitty looked so old, even her children who had come to greet Aunty Lizzie looked so much older than her own. They were all in their twenties and thirties.

Steele was very pleased to meet his cousins. He felt a little superior to them, maybe because of his height, his good looks or his fabulous education. "Steele wants to be an aviator", Lizzie told the family as they sat down to dinner "His father wants him to go to agricultural college and get a degree in farming, and set a record for the produce he can get from the farm."

The old man listened intently. Lizzie was so different from the others. The others had stayed nearer Ooty for the most part and kept in touch with John William. He felt Lizzie was not like them at all. She spoke differently. She too had that air of superiority. She didn't talk much about her husband, although John William felt he was partly responsible for her manner.

"You know of course I have eight children Papa, Steele who is the eldest has left school and Gerry wont be starting for another year or so. My daughter Ruth May will be coming to Madras to do nurses

training after she has finished her Senior Cambridge Exams. I don't know what the others will be doing, they are still too young."

"Have you seen Florence lately?" the old man asked. "Oh yes, she brings her little daughter Felicity to the Police lines and stays for many weeks at a time." Lizzie replied.

One day John William asked Lizzie if she would like to visit the gentlemen's club with him. "Do you remember when I taught you to play snooker at the club child?" "Yes, Papa, of course I do," she answered. "Well, .we can take Steele with us and I will introduce him to some of my very old friends"

Steele did not have to try hard to look his best. At eighteen, with stunning good looks, he simply had to put on a clean shirt and comb his hair, and grandpa would be very proud of him. "This is my grandson Steele", he said to all the old members, "He's going to be an aviator". Steele shook hands politely, and made small conversation with the gentlemen he was introduced to.

A bearer came up and bowed courteously to John William. "Your Lordship, what would you like to drink?" he asked. John William ordered his drink and a non-alcoholic drink for Lizzie and Steele. As a rule, women were not allowed in the gentlemen's club except on special occasions . Today was one such occasion.

Lizzie noticed again the snooker rules that were posted on the dining room wall, they were turning yellow with age She smiled to herself, she remembered how she first saw Locky across a snooker table more than twenty years ago. Her visit to Ooty lasted for a month. Gerry made himself at home and played all day with the children of the servants, running around and shouting and laughing in the large and interesting garden.

Steele accompanied his grand father on visits to his friends homes and to the markets. The old man was slow and leaned heavily on Steele. On Sundays they would order a rickshaw to take them to Church. Lizzie remembered this Church so well. It was here she received her first communion and here where she was confirmed. She did not genuflect this time to the Eternal Light, the Eternal Light of the world was now in her heart - always, and she could call on Him and pray wherever she happened to be.

Lizzie did not feel at one with her siblings. They had grown apart, she now felt a stranger amongst her own. Nobody spoke about their mother, and Lizzie could not bring herself to ask how she died.. One day she saw Steele looking at an old family photo, but before he could ask any questions she put her hand on him and pulled him away from the dining room wall on which the picture hung.

She did not want him to realize his grand mother was an Indian lest he'd come out with this information whilst conversing with his father.

Locky was still unaware that Lizzie's mother was an Indian, this was possibly the reason she never went to visit Ooty or to take him there.

After a few weeks, her visit came to an end. She put her arms around her father and hugged him, knowing full well it was the last time she would ever see him. "Goodbye Papa", she whispered, "May God bless you". She hid the tears that welled up into her eyes as she hastened towards the rickshaw. She waved to the other members of the family, "Goodbye, good bye, goodbye for always" .Steele looked at his mother's face wonderingly, she looked so sad. A boy of eighteen does not know what goes through the mind of his mother, Steele presumed it was because she was waving her family goodbye. He did not know about the time Lizzie met her mother in the streets of Calcutta and denied any knowledge of her.

In India, girls seemed to be second rate citizens, this also reflected the Victorian and Edwardian view of them. When they grew up, they would be sentenced to a life of domesticity, however talented they be. In Britain, women had been liberated. Bras were burned by the thousand. Should women aspire to being a writer, their books would be on good house keeping and the raising of children. Lizzie managed her house with business like skill. Her dozen or so servants were treated kindly and paid well according to the era, but never once would they be allowed to cross the line between servant and master.

Locky's magnificent size and appearance terrified most people ranging from the entire Central Province Police Force to the children who sat around his table. He was often heard to say, "Every one in the world is afraid of me, everyone except this little brown faced woman I am married to."

The dining table was always beautifully laid for each meal. Monogrammed cutlery with the initials ABL engraved on each piece was carefully laid out. Serviettes, starched and perfectly ironed always placed beside each china plate. If Locky was present, he sat at one end of the table while Lizzie sat at the other. Meal times were always fraught with tension. Conversation took the form of questions being fired at the children. They were afraid to open their mouths lest they gave the wrong answer.

"What is the shortest distance between two points", he threw this question out to them one day. No one dared to speak, the bearers who were serving dinner were always afraid they would be chastised for doing something wrong. "A straight line" ,piped up the youngest girl. Locky seemed to be surprised, not because she gave him the right answer, but because she had the guts to answer at all.

Lizzie often got quite cross with him for being so unbending, "Why cant you be more loving with them?" she would say. "Not so severe and austere." Flame their third daughter was really afraid of her father. She cowered and cringed each time she saw him, he would yell at her for being such a coward, which only made her worse. She would run and hide under the beds when she heard his footsteps in the house, her lovely curly hair getting caught in the springs under the bed.

Locky was an autocrat. He bullied his family, his servants, and shouted abuse to all the Indians who came into contact with him. Little children who played near his compound or in the street would be the recipient of his lashing tongue.

Even to drink a sip of water before finishing your meal was a reason to get shouted at. Thankfully the food at home was delicious. The children did not need telling twice to "eat up", they had been nine months at boarding school where the food was neither delicious or plentiful.

Four sets of deer's antlers adorned the dinning room wall. This was not usual, not even in India. Few people went shooting, and even fewer were successful at it. The Loughran children were raised on venison. Apart from the venison, they ate jungly moorghi and peafowl. Sometimes a large wild boar was shot and graced the table for the next few days.

Beef was difficult, if not impossible to obtain. The bull was the sacred vehicle of one of the Hindu Gods and as such, was not killed. Bulls were allowed to roam freely in the streets and market places and held precedence over people. If they ate the green vegetables piled up for sale, they were seldom shooed away., it was as if the vendor was supplying fuel for a Holy One. The country that boasted the greatest number of cattle in the world, was India.

Locky taught the boys to shoot. When they were about twelve years of age, he would take them out with him, arm them with a rifle and a lot of instructions. Lizzie was not altogether happy about this. She was so afraid one of them would be injured and worse than that killed by a wild animal or a stray bullet.

On one such occasion, the two middle brothers, Beatson and Alston went out with a couple of bullock cart wallas. The boys went by tonga to where the bullock cart was waiting for them. They transferred onto a pile of hay and sacking at the back of the bullock cart. After a few hours and miles, the cart trundled off the dusty road onto a track which was even more bumpy and dusty. They were now right in the middle of the jungle. Locky knew nothing of this adventure, they heard the sound of a motor bike in the distance, and thought it might be their father. The boys were afraid, and wished that he would come and look for them and rescue them from the jungle.

Alston was only about nine years old, while Beatson was no more than about fourteen. They got out of the cart and took a few steps away from it, going further into the undergrowth. Eyes were wide open and rifles were at the ready. The boys had no idea what they would encounter, maybe a deer or a peacock.

They heard the sound of rustling in the undergrowth. The bullock cart wallas remained near to the cart. The tension and fear was evident, although not a single word was spoken. Suddenly, and coming from nowhere, in the opposite direction to where they were pointing, they heard the loudest grunting of a huge, angry wild boar.

Beatson spun round and raised his rifle as it charged towards him. He took aim and fired his rifle. The bullet hit the wild boar which further angered the beast and added speed to its already furious charging.

He re-loaded and fired again, but alas too late. The wild boar drove its huge pointed tusk into the young boys thigh. His trousers were ripped as if they were made of paper, the blood pouring down his leg and into his shoe. The boar ran off. Alston and the bullock cart wallas tried to lift Beatson into the cart. Just as they were doing this, the boar turned, grunting and charging, began running towards them again.. Beatson's gun was loaded, he fired, and this time the boar fell, at his feet.

The bullock cart wallas were terrified, terrified of touching the dead animal, but more terrified of the outcome when the Burra Sahab saw what had happed to his son. Struggling, they lifted Beatson onto the hay and sacking and lay him down. The blood was pouring from his wound, the men did not know if he would live. They struggled and heaved until they laid the boar alongside the boy. Alston was crying, he climbed into the cart and sat between his brother and the boar. He tried very hard in his child like manner to comfort Beatson. The bullock cart hastened as best it could, bumping and banging its way to the road. The drivers were trying to avoid the deepest ruts in the track, so minimising the pain to the young lad. Beatson was trying to hide his tears. Locky had taught the boys that crying was not a man-thing, but try as he might, the tears were rolling down his young face.

The bullock cart reached the road. The drivers flagged down a public transport bus passing that way. The bus was held together with bits of string. Alston was only about nine years old and Beatson about thirteen.

After what seemed an eternity the bus stopped outside the Police House. Lizzie came running out as soon as she heard the bus. She almost fainted when she saw her precious son covered in blood. Nobody alive today remembers Locky's reaction. Beatson was rushed to the hospital where he was sewn up without anaesthetic, his screams could be heard throughout the town. He carried the great gash scar in his thigh all his life.

Locky's career in the police force as Inspector took him to many different towns in the Central Province. It was not unusual for the children to leave for school in March from one house only to return to another house and town a few hundred miles away., Jubulpur, Yeotmal, Nagpur, Seoni, Damoh.

Locky had joined the Police Force after working for a few years in the traditional occupation of his father, his grand father and his great grand father before him. He quit the railway leaving his younger brother to continue in the family tradition. His exemplary voice and bearing, and his British origin, immediately made him a candidate for a Chief Inspector in the police. When he gave an order every one jumped to it. If the command was not carried out immediately or perfectly, the offending Indian would know it.

On one such occasion, an Indian carpenter was employed to do some wood work, it might have been to make another gun rack for the Sahab. The Indian failed to work the wood exactly as Locky wanted, mind reading being part of the instructions. After all it was below his British dignity to speak at any length to an Indian. The following incident took place.

Locky was sitting reasonably close at hand, he was pulling through a rifle, a job he would entrust to nobody. The job meant dropping a piece of weighted string down the barrel of the gun, attached to the other end of the string was a bundle of soft cotton material, he'd then up end the gun and pull the weight through , so causing the ensuing cotton bundle to clean the barrel of the gun.

He saw the mistake the Indian carpenter had made, he turned the gun round so that the barrel pointed towards his own chest, then sharply without a word he struck the Indian with the butt of the gun, right in the middle of his puny chest.

The Indian fell backwards and was thoroughly winded. On seeing what he'd done and feeling extremely sorry and guilty about it, he rolled up a five rupee not and shoved it into an empty cartridge case and threw it at the carpenter. Locky could not bring himself to apologise for this rough and bullying act. The weak, winded carpenter picked up the cartridge, extracted the note, touched his head in thanks and continued his work.

Another time, one of the bearers was caught trying to steal sugar. The servant tipped sugar into a cup and then covered it with a thin film of tea, thinking perhaps to pour the tea off later and dry the sugar or use it as it was in his own drink at his home.. Locky saw what the servant was doing, he swung his arm out to hit him across the face. The servant moved closer to the Sahab to try and avoid the striking blow, where upon Locky's arm flew round the servants neck. He pulled the man towards him and bit him really hard on the cheek. Ruth May was a witness to this awful act and could remember the teeth marks in the servants face, to this day.

You never heard a Hindu complaining of his lot in life, the total resignation to their status and caste was in the hands of their God. There was no envy or anger expressed, no discontent because there were others higher up in the caste system than himself, no pride because you were higher up than someone else. What a quality to possess, contentment in what so ever state you were. Understanding like this often takes a life time to acquire, if at all.

At the same time when all this was taking place at home, a man by the name of Mohandas Gandhi was becoming head line news. He was a Hindu by religion, born in South Africa and educated in England. By profession he was a barrister. On his return to South Africa he was appalled by the state of colour discrimination that effected every body. White South Africans were descendants from European countries, the blacks were native South Africans and the coloureds were Indians or any one who had mixed blood in them.

Public transport, hospitals and schools, places of work and recreational areas were strictly separated. You didn't dare go into a white area, market place, or otherwise if you had any Indian or African blood in you. Often there were riots and fights when batons and canes were wielded , injuries frequently sustained and many fatal incidents occurred.

None of the Loughrans ever went to South Africa, somewhere along the line they had Indian blood in them, although Locky never found quite where. India too was in turmoil, they struggled for independence from British rule. There was talk of separation , the two religions in India each wanting a part of the country when independence was finally given. How on earth does one separate a country when people of the Hindu and Moslem faiths lived in all places in India.

People were tired of the Empire, making the local Indians look as if they were second class citizens, and continuing to insist that the

British were far superior to any one else on earth. There were riots and uprisings, this time not because of the various shades of colour , but of different religions. Moslems and Hindus, whilst brothers in the great sub-continent wanted self-rule from the British as well as from each other.

Mohandas Gandhi was a pacifist, discouraging fighting and encouraging the local people to adopt the spinning genny hand weaving spindle as their symbol of strength, peace and independence. Up till now, the spinning industry in the north of England dominated the textile world. Vast quantities of cotton was purchased from Egypt, U.S.A., and India, transported by steamer and then by canal barges up to the great industrial north of England, to dozens of weaving sheds in the large towns of the north. In Lancashire places like Blackburn, Burnley and Bolton, in Yorkshire places like Rochdale, Todmorden and Halifax, to name but a few.

The finely woven cotton was then exported to Egypt, the United States and to India. This provided employment for thousands of workers in Britain. Young children, often no older than ten years of age would walk miles in all kinds of .weather to earn a small wage, hours were long and exhausting, but, there was plenty of employment for all those who wanted it - until the arrival of Gandhi.

Resentment among the mill owners grew as India began weaving cotton for herself. As decades passed during the middle and late twentieth century, fewer and fewer mills remained open. The law in Britain now forbade children under a certain age to work in the mills, compulsory education rose to the age of fourteen.

The world was becoming smaller, the arrival of the passenger aeroplane and the motor car made almost all the places on the globe more easily accessible. No more the slow boat to China, the day of the tea clippers had long since passed. Vast liners were transporting people to the far corners of the earth. Migration amongst Anglo Indians became a necessity. The unjust and greedy acts purported to have taken place by the British towards the Indians, was causing unrest amongst all peoples..

The caste system which had been part of life in India was slowly being brought out before the eyes of the world.

Outcastes, that group of people, lower than the lowest castes created by the Aryans, centuries before, were now renamed The Children of God. Mohandas Gandhi was a character to be reckoned with. A character much loved and much hated. Several attempts had been made on his life during the decades before independence, attempts that had been unsuccessful.

One day in January nineteen forty eight, the Loughrans were at home on the farm listening to a battery run radio when the fateful news was broadcast that Mohandas Gandhi, the Mahatma, the Teacher had been assassinated. It was received in stunned silence, the family little understood the political impact this incident would have on the nation as a whole, nor how the ripples would be felt for decades to come.

Riots broke out every where. Trains were being bombarded with weapons of wood, stone and metal, carriages and their passengers being burnt alive. Scores of villages were set alight, and people were afraid to venture out into the towns, villages, and cities. The old India was divided. It was the year nineteen forty seven. Pakistan, the home of the Moslems was born, it was the fourteenth day of August. The very next day, India was given independent rule from Britain, Hindustan became the home of the Hindus.

The Indian scholars who journeyed to the hill stations from all four corners of the country were instructed to keep their surnames off the tin trunks which carried their school uniforms and belongings. Surnames often gave away one's identity and religion. If a train or bus was attacked, and the names of one of the scholars trunks happened to be of the opponents religion, it could or would be disastrous for the teachers and scholars travelling in that group. If however, your name happened to be Gerald Smith, John William Cranston or Gerry Loughran, it didn't matter, these were so obviously British names that students were not under any threat.

On arriving at the hill station, seven thousand feet up in the foothills of the Himalayas, one felt far removed from the unrest that threatened to engulf the rest of the sub-continent. Life continued in school as usual.

Wynberg-Allen was a beautiful school, a cluster of buildings with the main hall built like a vast ship. It rose three stories high and the front had an apex roof which gave it a grand and imposing appearance. The lesser buildings comprised the Cambridge Block class rooms and a section called Constantia which contained the Kindergarten class rooms and the junior dormitories. When the boys reached a certain age they went to Allen, the boys school, situated on a neighbouring mountain, perched high on a peak with unrivalled views of the Doon Valley and the mighty River Ganges which glistened in the sunlight as it wove its way across the country.

The scenery was breath takingly beautiful, when dusk fell and the detail of the mountains disappeared from view, you were enthralled by the sunsets, changing in colour and design by the minute until the sun sank below the horizon.

The mountain ranges in the opposite direction were covered by perpetual snows. The peaks glistened in the sunlight even when the temperature rose to a comfortable seventy and eighty degrees in mid summer. Is it no wonder the Hindus believed the home of their Gods was in the Himalayas?

Many, many years later, the writer took her twenty one year old daughter to visit the sights of India, amongst which , and of paramount importance was the citation of her old school. "You never told us you were educated in such a beautiful place", her young daughter said to her." Oh yes darling, for twenty one years I told you but no one believed me."

Nineteen forty nine was a good year at school, the older siblings were leaving, having completed their Cambridge Examinations. It was round about this time that Locky had decided enough was enough. He'd retire from the Police and take up his life on the farm which his parents had bought years before as an investment property. It was a forty acre holding lying outside the small town of Damoh where he had been the

Chief Inspector for the past few years. He was having trouble with pains in his chest and because his father had died at an early age as a result of his heart condition, it was thought best that Locky should stop his police work.

He was still a young man, at forty five he looked and felt good. On the first of January nineteen forty nine Locky went on a News Years day shoot. His old friend George Bernard Shaw accompanied him. They brought home a deer which would supply meat for both their families for a few days. They dragged the animal into the back compound where the servants would gut and skin it in the hours of daylight. Lizzie and the children were already in bed and asleep when he finally went to bed. Before long, he rose from his bed and went outside into the dark to get a breath of air, he was finding it hard to breathe because of the severe pain he felt in his chest.

After a while he returned, only to find the claustrophobic area of his bedroom was more than he could bare. He sat on the edge of his bed trying to relieve the pain he was feeling, but to no avail. He stood in the doorway and leaned against the doorpost because he felt his legs could not support him any longer.

Lizzie heard him moving about and got up to see what the matter was. He looked sallow and was sweating profusely. Lizzie had never seen her strong and handsome husband in this condition before. She knew something was seriously wrong. She hastened to awake Beatson and told him to cycle to the American Doctor's house and ask him to attend Locky.

It was pitch dark, there was no electricity on the farm and consequently no street lights for the two miles or so to the Doctor's house. Young Beatson rode as fast as he could, hoping the Doctor would come and solve the problem with his dad, and fearing in his young mind that this would not be possible.

Locky was breathing very heavily, murmuring that the crushing pain in his chest would not permit him to lie down. He felt dizzy, and held on to Lizzie leaning heavily on her small frame. When the Doctor heard the news he threw Beatson's bike into the back of the jeep, Beatson jumped in beside the doctor, who drove as fast as the bumpy road would permit. On arrival at the farm he got out of the vehicle and gently and calmly helped Locky to his bed, where he gave him medication that would ease the pain in his chest and allow him to sleep.

When all was quiet, Beatson returned to his bed and went to sleep. The Doctor walked out onto the veranda with Lizzie and in hushed tones he explained to her what had caused this pain. "It is very serious Mrs.Loughran," he said. "As far as I can determine at the moment, he has a clot of blood near his heart causing obstruction and an attack, if he should make it for the next fortnight, his body responding to the mediation I am giving him, he will be alright, but the crisis will occur after the course of medication ceases, in about two weeks time."

Lizzie said goodbye to him and thanked him deeply for his care and concern. The Doctor was a friend of the family and would visit more times than duty required to ensure Locky received the best attention he could give. Lizzie said nothing of this to her husband. She told the orderly to go to the post office and send a telegram to Steele, to come home soon, as Locky is seriously ill. The second telegram was sent to her sister Florence who was a nurse living in secrecy with her English husband in Calcutta. "Come soon, Locky ill."

Steele arrived by motor bike and Florence by train and tonga. The days dragged on .. The children were told to be quiet and play away in the compound. Silence enveloped the farm., Gerry who was only seven, and Amela at eleven sensed that something was really going to happen. Lizzie hardly spoke to them, she went about with a face they barely recognised, so sad and deep in thought.

On the morning of the fourteenth, Steele was in Locky's bedroom when Florence came to give him his medication. Steele helped his father to sit up while he took the glass of water from Florence, he swallowed one tablet, handed the glass back to her and lay back in Steele's arms. His head fell onto his son's arm and his eyes closed. Steele lay his father back on the pillows, realizing at once that he had died. He did not remove his arms from around his body, he just lowered himself and knelt beside the bed and felt the tears running down his face.

Florence went in search of Lizzie who was organising the servants about meals for the day. "Come Lizzie, my darling sister" she said, "The news is bad, I'm so sorry to tell you Locky is dead."

Lizzie was hysterical, she ran outside and shouted up to the God who she believed in, lifting her eyes, heart , hands and voice heavenward , she cried, again and again, "Oh God, what am I to do without him, Oh God what am I to do without him, Oh God What am I to do without him.?

Chapter 9
Call back from death

Doctor Rice was called and confirmed and certified Locky's death. Steele drove to Jubulpur to warn Locky's mother that he would be coming to her home but to expect the worst, so preparing her for the news of his death. Lizzie, shaking with nerves and unable to calm herself, accompanied the body of her dearly beloved husband on the sixty four mile journey to Jubulpur, where he would be buried in the cemetery alongside his father, his sister and many of his relatives.

Amela remembers the body of her dead father being carried out on a stretcher, it was the first time she had seen a dead body, and she remembers being frightened. She did not cry however, because even at the tender age of eleven, she felt no great loss.

Florence was left at the farm to take care of the children and to run the household. Flame held Amela's hand, she said nothing, Gerry at the age of seven could not really understand the finality of death. There was a subdued atmosphere in the house, no one spoke about death, no more fun and games, no pleasure in play , every one just waited for the return of their mother after the funeral. What would happen now?

The farm at Damoh was a few miles out of the town. It was totally isolated, surrounded by pastures alternating from green and verdant during the monsoon to dry and barren through the months of April and May, until the monsoon rains arrived mid June. The population of Damoh, some forty five thousand inhabitants, were almost without exception Indians, some practising the faith of Hindus or Moslems who had not gone into the newly founded country of Pakistan. There were also a number of Indian Christians who attended the Christian Church. Lizzie did not attend the Church because she nor the children could understand Hindi. Apart from the two American missionary families and the Loughrans, no one else in Damoh spoke English as their first language.

In a couple of months the children would go to boarding school again. Beatson had completed his Senior Cambridge Exams and could help run the farm until it was decided what Lizzie would do with it. She did not want to stay in Damoh where she would be totally alone for most of the time. The domestic servants would continue to attend the household chores and the preparation of the meals, the gardeners would see to the gardens, and the field workers would attend to the cattle and the sowing and harvesting of crops.

Lizzie felt the burden of her life almost impossible to bear, yet within her was her own natural strength and her faith in God which reminded her of the Scripture verse which read, "As thy day, so shall thy strength be."

Lizzie decided to sell the farm. Steele had returned to his job in the Air Force, and Ruth May was in the South of India studying to be a nurse. She could not allow Beatson to give up his life to run the farm, it was acceptable until such time as a purchaser was found for the property. When Locky had taken over the deeds from his parents, he had decided to register the farm in Gerry's name to avoid previous owners from causing trouble, and disputing ownership in the unlikely event of his death.

Buyers soon became interested in the farm, but as soon as they realised the property was registered in the name of a minor, they lost interest. Lizzie kept reducing the price more and more , hoping some trusting purchaser would take on the farm and not fear the transfer of ownership.

Several years passed. Beatson stayed at home and ran the farm. It was during this time when both Lizzie and her son began to study the scriptures in great depth. The teachings of the Bible proved to be a life changing experience for both of them, and for many people who came in contact with them later in their lives.

The three middle children went back to school but as soon as their education was complete they sailed away to a country where they could be understood and where they could find careers and partners in life. By this time Florence 's English husband had sent her ahead of him to purchase a property in England and prepare a home for him and their daughter after his retirement. He would then be able to openly own her as his wife. For many years he had to keep her hidden to avoid the Bank for which he worked finding out that he had married a "native" a person born in India, which was against their rules.

Marie Louise, Alston and Flame soon settled in England. Marie Louise and Alston joined the forces and sent money to Lizzie to help pay for the running of the farm and other expenses which had to be met. Beatson too went to England against his own wishes, he wanted to stay on the farm and take care of his mother, but Lizzie insisted he went with the others and took care of them.

Lizzie had finally found a purchaser for the farm, a man who was prepared to take her word that no one would ever return to claim the farm as their own. It had taken four years to do this, Gerry was now eleven and Amela fifteen, they were the last to remain with her because they were the youngest. The sale would not be completed until April, but in case it fell through as so many of the others had done previously, she decided to send them back to school.

Those last few weeks on the farm brought them closer together than ever before. Every thing was looking hopeful, the family would soon be reunited, each with new jobs and a new English home.

It was a very warm night that night in early March nineteen fifty four. The servants had carried the beds out onto the threshing floor and had made them up with mosquito nets and light cotton sheets . At dusk, they went to their own homes in the village opposite and in the centre of Damoh to their own families, leaving Lizzie, Amela and Gerry by themselves. A lantern had been lit and the family prepared to go to bed. It was very nice to sleep under the stars, but before doing so, Lizzie made sure the house was locked up. Gerry carried the lantern and the three of them went round the house to bolt all the doors leading to the outside of the house.

Amela shut and bolted the doors, but something terrible happened when she came to the last one. She put her hand on the wooden frame to help close the door, her hand slipped off the wooden frame and went straight through the pane of glass by the side, on extracting her hand from the broken pane, she caught her wrist on a jagged piece of glass that was still attached to the frame.

A spurt of blood came gushing out of Amela's hand. She did not know what had happened. She felt no pain. She moved her hand in a gesture trying to find the source of the fountain of blood, on doing so, the blood gushed out splattering every thing within two or three feet of where she stood.

"Oh my God", Lizzie murmured, trying to keep the panic out of her voice. "Gerry, take the lantern and run across to the nearest village and tell the servant there to fetch a tonga from the town, hurry, hurry, tell them that the missi babba has cut her hand." Gerry forgot that he was afraid of the dark and ran as fast as his legs would take him. He knew this was a matter of extreme urgency, and that his sister was bleeding to death. Lizzie hastened and tied a tourniquet on Amela's upper arm, picked up the torch and hastened after Gerry. Amela held her left forearm with her right hand as high as she could and proceeded to follow Lizzie. "Its alright, Mum" Amela was trying to reassure Lizzie, "it doesn't hurt." The blood was pouring down her night dress and into her shoes as she proceeded to walk on the dark and dusty road. She could feel it congealing on her arms before dripping off her elbows. Her night dress was soaked from the neck line to its hem, she could feel the blood squelching in her shoes.

Lizzie knew her daughter had cut her main artery and unless the bleeding was stemmed she would lose her life. They could see the tonga in the distance. Lizzie was silently praying that the doctor would be available and that her daughter would live. "Please God, Please God, Please God," that's all she could think of saying.

On arriving at the house of the doctor, he took one look at Amela and said nothing, just pointed to the hospital, a tiny building some fifty yards away from his house. Amela was lead into a small operating theatre and a mask of chloroform was put over her face. "Count sheep," said the doctor.

Lizzie stayed by her daughter's side until she noticed the girl had stopped breathing, then in panic she ran out of the theatre. Gerry was sitting outside on a bench in the corridor and witnessed his mother in this state. He began to cry inconsolably. "Is she going to die Mum?" he sobbed, "I don't want her to die Mum."

Inside the theatre, the doctor left Amela's extended arm and began trying to start her heart beating . He pumped her chest again and again, then a few minutes later Amela's heart responded and began beating on its own accord. There was heard a sigh of relief, he did not speak to the nurse who was assisting him, he just sighed, allowed her to wipe his forehead, and continued with the job of sewing her up again. He had called her back from death. He made a small cut up from the gash in her wrist and pulled down the radial artery which had sprung apart in the accident. When he had joined the two severed ends, he sewed it up with numerous stitches.. He set about clearing the blood off the rest of her body, and dressing her in a hospital gown. When he emerged after what seemed an eternity he placed his hand on Lizzie's shoulder, "Your daughter will be alright Mrs.Loughran," he said. "Your prayers have been answered." She could barely speak but through her tears, she held the Doctor's hand and whispered, "How could I ever thank you?"

The nurse wheeled Amela into a small recovery room, and placed a chair beside the bed for Gerry " Sit and watch over her". Lizzie told him. "Tell Amela the moment she comes round that I will not be long, I've gone home to clean up. She will be coming home in the morning."

Lizzie took a tonga and went to the home of two of the servants and together they rode to the farm. The sight that greeted them sent shivers done Lizzie's spine. It was a night mare, how could any one lose so much blood and still be alive. The servants heated water and together they began scrubbing the floors and removing any trace of the accident. Lizzie did not want Amela to see any of the frightening mess that looked as if a headless chicken had run through the farm.

Next morning Amela went to the door of the Doctor's surgery , she sat first in line to see him. Next to her, but sitting on the floor, was a man whose hands and feet were bandaged with the same brown coloured bandages that now were wrapped round Amela's hand. She noticed that his feet were much smaller than they should have been for his size. His hands too seemed to be so badly disfigured, almost as if he had no fingers. The man was a leper.

Lizzie went in to the Doctor's surgery to hear what his prognosis was. "Your daughter has lost half her blood supply, Mrs Loughran, but because of her superior strength and size, she will be able to make it up before too long. She will suffer no ill effects as a result of the accident." He shook Lizzie's hand and bade the two of them farewell.

The relief that flooded over Lizzie is hard to describe. It was four years since Locky's death, she had made a life for herself and her children, calling on her inner resources to see her through times of trouble, but somehow this was different. A mother is a broken human being at the loss of a child, her God carried her through this day, as her day so was her strength. God had his hand on Amela, her life was mapped out in his master plan, Amela was grateful.

On her return home, the servants lined the threshing floor to greet her. They put their hands together in salutation and then bent down to touch her feet. "Missi Babba, Missi babba," they kept repeating the phrase. Her recovery was better than anticipated. After a three week lapse, the stitches had to be removed. Because of the accident and the now confirmed sale of the farm, Amela and Gerry did not return to school. They were going to spend a few months with their Grandmother in Jubulpur whilst awaiting the departure date of the liner Stratheden on which they had booked a passage to England.

Chapter 10
Wynberg Allen

Steele The Aviator.

"Second to none in the country" are the words used on the internet to describe Wynberg Allen. The school was chosen by Locky and Lizzie for the education of all their children. Gerald Smith and his wife Marie Baker, who had no children of their own had invested a huge sum of money for their education . The total sum sufficient to educate Steele right down to Gerry. The school was a prestigious English boarding school which offered the finest education to scholars who came from the far corners of the country, Ceylon and Africa.

Locky and Lizzie had eight children.

Steele was steel. An exceptional character. Being the eldest in the family, he had left school before some of the younger ones even started. His artistic ability and his sportsmanship singled him out above his peers. In his final year at school, he was asked to paint the banner for his house, which would be carried in the sports day march past.

Having done that, the other three houses in the boy's school, asked him to paint their banners also. Word soon got round to the girls school, and before long he found himself painting all four banners for Allen, Foy, Powell and West house. Ruth May , Flame and Amela were all in West house. The banner of an eagle in flight with the motto nil des perandum, painted in gold on blue satin was so beautiful it was used for sports days, years after Steele had painted it. In nineteen fifty three, two of the banner bearers were Flame and Amela, proudly exhibiting their brother Steele's art work.

Sports day in school was a triumph for Steele. He excelled in pole vaulting and running. He made himself a bamboo pole for his vaulting, there is picture in his archives of a teen age Steele flying through the air, legs upwards defying gravity. He held the school record.

When he left school he spent quality time with his father, he was the only one of the eight siblings who did so. Locky taught him to hunt, to swim and to fish. One wonders if his close tie with his normally distant father, harkened back to the time in Calcutta, when as a tiny baby, the big strong man held the little scrap in his arms, and sang the words of the song "Little pal, when daddy's gone away."

Steele went to agricultural college, so he could run the farm in Damoh. Two years learning about fertilizers, ploughing and counter ploughing, so as the wheat could stand six feet high in the fields, again showing his exceptional talent in what ever he chose to do.

In January nineteen forty nine he came home after receiving a wire from Lizzie, "Come home Locky very ill." It was Steele who held Locky in his arms when he took the final medication, when he handed the tumbler back to Florence then fell back into Steele's arms. Locky had been so proud to hold Steele in his arms when at his christening he handed him to the priest, and this day, Steele held Locky in his arms, as he took his final breath.

Plans changed considerably after Locky's death. Ruth May was in Madras doing nurses training. She married a man who was visiting his sister in hospital, and had fallen in love with her and proposed marriage. As a result she did not complete her training. Steele forgot all about agriculture and became what he always wanted to be, an aviator.

He joined the Indian Air Force as a cadet, and very soon climbed the ladder to be a Squadron Leader and a Fighter Pilot. Amela remembers in her final year at school, seeing a tiger moth or some other one man aeroplane, swooping and diving, circuiting and bumping over the

Wynberg sports ground. Every one in school heard of Steele's success, and Flame and Amela basked in their big brothers display.

Beatson, who had completed his Senior Cambridge Exam, took on the job of taking care of the farm and his mother. The five younger ones continued in School, the education of all being paid for by Gerald Smith.

Steele was a huge success in the Indian Air Force. He rose to Commander in the 37th fighter Squadron and received a medal of bravery for his courage. This medal was only awarded to very few men. He married and brought his bride to the farm to meet Lizzie. The custom in India was to have a huge reception to welcome the new bride into the family. Lizzie met this obligation by inviting all the servants, the field workers and the casual workers like the dhobi, the gardeners etc. to a huge feast on the farm.

Some two hundred people arrived, from different religions and from different castes. As the Hindu caste system forbade people of different castes from eating together, Lizzie supplied vegetables, spices, rice, oil and flour in large quantities to each family. Small choolas were made all around the farm. One can best describe a choolah as a U shaped barbeque, filled with pieces of fire wood, which were either pulled out or pushed in to regulate the temperature at which the food could be cooked. The food was prepared separately by each family and eaten separately, each person ensuring they did not touch or were not touched by any other person in the crowd.

After this unusual reception, Steele returned to his life in the air force. He was posted high up in the Himalayas and to other Air force bases in major cities. Apart from his duties as a test pilot and a fighter pilot there were numerous competitions going on. Of course Steele entered most, if not all of them. As a result he held the international gliding record for many, many years covering a distance of about two hundred and sixty seven miles in a glider with no engine.

Strange as it may seem to the outside world, the Himalayas, although the highest mountain range in the world, did not have a reputation as skiing country. Steele went in for the international winter sports. One of the events he entered and won was the slalom, where he raced between obstacles, left and right, right and left, all the time descending down the mountain at a break neck speed.

Alston who himself was a sportsman in squash and golf winning trophy after trophy, was unable to balance on skis, it was awfully amusing listening to his description of skis in the days when Steele was champion: "They looked like floor boards " he said, "great flat wide, no style floor boards, with hiking boots strapped to them". Just how true this was, only a skier can tell.

Steele designed the Indian Air force logo. He was decorated for his bravery in other combats also.

Steele's marriage failed and after many years they divorced. Their three children were raised in India and seldom saw their English cousins, children of Beatson, Alston, Flame, Amela and Gerry. Steele joined the commercial Air India airline. He was scheduled to fly many of the world's dignitaries from their home counties to the commonwealth and America, top politicians who were on international political journeys, also sportsmen, actors, film directors and royalty. He has a host of pictures taken of himself with George Bush senior, Maggie Thatcher, President Mobarak , President Nasser, Pundit Nehru, Indira Ghandi, the famous film director David Bean and the actor Sean Connery who he was often mistaken for, and many, many more.

He was very conscious of colour, and was often heard to describe an Indian as blue eyed, fair haired and with an European complexion, suggesting almost as if a dark skinned , dark eyed person was inferior.

When Lizzie and the six younger children settled in Britain, she thought she'd never see him again. Steele re-married, this time to a beautiful Air Hostess, a gorgeous woman who was conversant in many subjects, whose international travel had made her a fount of wisdom in cultural matters, ranging from the caste system in India to the normal day to day life in the United States of America. They had one son, who they lovingly called Junior.

Steele did not attend any of the family functions, firstly because he lived in India, Singapore, Malta or Ceylon. When he removed to

England, he seemed to be occupied with his old Air force buddies and friends and was sadly missed at each family wedding and re-union.

It was really sad when Lizzie was dying, all she cried for, hoped and longed for was her son Steele. He was her first born and she asked for him again and again. Was it because she remembered Steele holding Locky on his deathbed, that she longed to see him one more time. Lizzie knew she would lose her battle against cancer.

His knowledge of the background history of the Loughran family was paramount. Because he was the oldest he could remember things the younger ones could not. He furnished the writer with birth, marriage and death certificates, of characteristics of grandparents, of Locky and of John William who he was privileged to meet when he was about eighteen years old.

It was he who described the photo on the Dining Room Wall in the aristocratic John William's home. It was Steele who went to the gentlemen's club with his grand father and heard members of the club address the old man as "Your Lordship". It was he who sold the tiger skins in Calcutta, who hunted deer and panther with him, who swam with him and who helped to renovate the farmhouse in Damoh.

Oh yes, Steele was special, he was steel, and as such, seldom would he let any one look into the windows of his soul. Much of the family history was furnished by him, much of it came from the internet. Imagine the surprise of the researcher, when looking up famous Anglo Indians found listed Loughran. I.S. Commander of the 37th Squadron (Night Fighters) Indian Air Force. The Researcher telephoned Steele to let him know what he had found. Steele knew nothing about the entry. Towards the latter part of his life, Amela often visited Steele and his hospitable wife. They lived in a cute bungalow with a lovely garden that responded to the tender loving care of Marlene. The house overlooked the beautiful Epsom Downs, research showed this to be the most desirable place to live in the U.K., when it came to crime and trouble, Epsom came out tops.

Steele still missed India, he missed his air force pals he missed the farm, the hunting, the fishing, the swimming. He missed his father, his back ground, the many police homes he shared with Locky. He missed the care from the bearers, the orderlies, the dhobis and the malis. He missed his youth. He was much older than Amela when he re-located to England, and it is possible the mental change was too difficult for him to make.

Rex remembers an incident that happened during one of Steele's visits to England when he was flying for a commercial airline. Amela had not long passed her driving test and offered to give Steele a lift to the place where he intended to visit. It was the first time he was a passenger in a car driven by a woman, to cap it all a young woman, who was his little sister.

"Amela" he said, " don't forget to keep the white line to the right of the car, its not an aeroplane you know, where the white line is the place you keep in front of the nose of the plane." It took him years to realize that women were capable and responsible creatures, rather more than attractive ornaments.

Steele had flown the aeroplane which had taken Ruth May to Australia where she'd settled in very nicely into a new home. He often saw her and her children and helped her a great deal during difficult times.

Now it is nineteen eighty, and Amela was inviting all members of the family to her farm in the Pennines to welcome Ruth May on her first visit to England. Would Steele be there?

Ruth May The Soprano

Ruth May left home after completing her Senior Cambridge Examinations to take up a nurses training course in the Central Hospital in Madras, South India. At the time this was the only hospital in India which offered a training programme that was recognised as qualification for employment any where in the world.

Ruth May and Steele were closer to each other not only in age but in friendship also. They played together as little ones and consequently shared the same memories. Ruth May was nine years old when the youngest of the four sisters was born, and unlike her father, was delighted the baby was a girl. She was permitted the privilege of choosing a name for the baby, she named her Amela. She would carry the baby about as if she were a doll, often singing her to sleep with her two finger pressed lightly on the baby's eyes in an effort to keep them closed until the little one was asleep.

Ruth May was very intelligent, and sailed through her school exams effortlessly, talented in sport but more so in her ability to sing powerfully and in perfect tune. Her father recognised this, being a wonderful singer himself, and began giving her singing lessons. He was often heard to instruct her to breathe deeply, pitch her voice, sing up, stand up straight, imagine the audience is sitting fifty yards away from you, now sing to them.

Her teenage voice developed in tone and power If the school choir needed a soloist it was Ruth May who filled the roll. Her talent carried her through life. When she was training to be a nurse, she joined the Church Choir, and several other musical organisations and was soon picked out to be their lead singer. During the celebrations of India's Independence, she was chosen to sing a solo to the huge celebrating gathering, she was only eighteen years of age. She lifted her voice and heeded the instruction she had received since she was a very young girl. She could hear Locky's voice saying to her, "Lift your voice, breathe deeply, imagine the audience is fifty yards away from you, now sing to them."

Her voice rang out clear and strong:

> *"I saw a peaceful old valley,*
> *With a carpet of corn for the floor,*
> *And I heard a voice within me, whisper,*
> *This is worth fighting for.*
> *Didn't I build that cabin,*
> *Didn't I plant that corn,*
> *Didn't my loved ones before me,*
> *Fight for this country, before I was born.*
> *I gathered my loved ones around me,*
> *I gazed at each face I adore,*
> *And I heard a voice within me thunder,*
> *THIS IS WORTH FIGHTING FOR.*

For the rest of her lifetime, this song would be associated with her, and her alone.

It was during this time, she noticed a very tall and handsome man visiting one of the patients in the hospital. He had seen and noticed too the lovely young nurse who was attending his relative. The man, who was in his middle thirties, was an athlete, a runner who had made a name for himself. He asked her to go to the pictures with him, Ruth May was flattered, never having had any previous experience of men and love affairs, she accepted the invitation and Humphrey began courting the teenager.

She soon fell in love with him, and accepted his proposal of marriage. Ruth May was only nineteen and needed the permission of her parents to go ahead with the wedding. She wrote to Lizzie requesting that Locky would give the permission . Lizzie replied that she should go ahead and get married, Lizzie herself having given her consent, and after the marriage that she would inform Locky of the union. Due to family and farm commitments, no member of the Loughran family were present at the wedding. Very soon after Ruth May fell pregnant and Locky was informed of the marriage and the expected baby.

It was round about this time, he felt the pangs of pain in his chest, he would never have given his permission to Ruth May, she was too young and was there any man on earth good enough to marry his daughter? She never completed her nurses training, but after marriage gave her whole hearted attention to looking after her growing family. Very soon after her first daughter was born, she had a second child, another little girl. Her husband was disappointed it was not a boy just as Locky had been each time he had a daughter. Ruth May went on to have another two daughters, making it a total of four now. Her in laws and all Humphries relatives were very disappointed, could this reaction be a sign of Victorian or Edwardian times or was it the on going and continuing desire of Indian fathers and fathers in law to favour having a son more than a daughter.

Her life in Madras was very different to the life of her mother Lizzie. Ruth May worked non stop in the home, she prepared all the food for the family, did all the sewing of the children's clothes, did all the housework, the shopping , the gardening and taking care of the children without the help of servants and ayahs. Not only that, but she had to wrestle with the problem of communicating with the native Indians because the language in South India was Tamil, and she had been used to talking to the servants in Central India in the native language which was Hindi.

Her live was not easy, she always seemed to be pregnant or breast feeding, there was no time for her to develop as a beautiful woman herself, she lost her youthful bloom and found herself pregnant again. This time, much to the relief of her husband and in laws she gave birth to a baby boy. She called him Loughran. She was barely thirty years of age when she gave birth to her sixth child, another little girl, whom she called Lizzie.

Ruth May felt alone and cut off from her family, the ones she grew up with, her father had died and her mother and siblings were starting a new life in England. Her husband, who worked in the railway, was not the companion she had hoped, not the friend who she could share the hardship of life with.

She got the kids into a first class boarding school in the Nilgiris, not too far from the plantation that John William once owned. She had never met John William, he had long since died anyway, and only Steele and Gerry had ever been to visit him with their mother Lizzie. Her life now revolved around her own little Locky and Lizzie, and the four older girls who turned out to be the joy in her life.

Ruth May was standing on the quay side alongside the ship H.M.S Stratheden. She had two little children by her side, she looked up to the passengers standing on the deck, hundreds of them who waved to people who stood beside her. She caught sight of her mother, Amela and Gerry, the tears were streaming down her thin sad face, she waved, trying hard to dry her tears at the same time. She knew she would never see her mother again, maybe Amela and Gerry, but never her mother again. The great liner slowly left the harbour , leaving her alone and desolate.

Ruth May was not much more than thirty years of age, her hair was beginning to thin, her face sagged, there was little evidence of the bloom of youth that once made her such a beauty. Her husband failed to notice how sad she was, how lifeless and tired she was. She went back to Madras and resumed her life as best she could, until Steele came to visit her one day. "What's the point in staying here sister," he asked, people are emigrating to the new world, life is easier in England, "Why don't you consider it?" Ruth May gave it much thought until she decided to do as Steele suggested. Humphrey's family had gone to Australia and they were going to sponsor Ruth May and the whole of her family to go there.

The upheaval must have been horrendous, but the thrill came when Steele was the pilot of the plane that flew them to Melbourne. She was re-united with her sister in law, and Humphrey's brother who was married to one of Ruth May's cousins. At last she had met one of the blood relations belonging to her mother Lizzie's family. Cousin Philo remembered John William, and the Indian grandmother who she said always wore a sari and kept her place in the kitchen.

Poor Pushpa, she had been brought up to serve her husband and family and right through her life she maintained that servitudal manner until she died in early middle age. Could her children, Lizzie in particular, see her as anything but an Indian servant. It would be very difficult for the reader to understand how deep colour consciousness, British superiority or Indian inferiority is felt and how near impossible it is to genuinely dismiss it.

Ruth May's life took a turn upwards. Australia is a wonderful country. Her children all pursued careers as stock brokers, teachers and health consultants and carers while raising grandchildren for her. Her marriage failed, she had separated from Humphrey. She wrote to Lizzie and the others frequently, shortage of money did not permit her to make the long journey to visit her mother and siblings. In the days of the early sixties, telephones only belonged to those with money, so telecommunication was not like it is today. Lizzie died, sadly Ruth May remembered the last time she saw her beloved mother, when she stood on the quay side waving to her, in a final goodbye.

It was nineteen eighty now, twenty six years had passed since she last saw Amela, Today she was going to England for the great Loughran family re-union and their Memories of the Raj.

Beatson The Man of God.

Beatson stood beside Lizzie for the first two years of her widowhood.

Although he was her second son, he truly was the head of the family, putting the needs of his mother and siblings before his own. When Locky died, he resumed all responsibility for the farm and the continued education of the younger members of the family. It was whilst he was on the farm during the long days and lonely evenings that he developed an interest in the Word of God. He was often seen behind a yoke of oxen, ploughing the field whilst holding a Bible in his hand, reading and studying the intricate revelations to be found within its pages.

Evenings were spent with his mother, by the dim light of the kerosene lamp, discussing what they had read, and praying together for revelations. They were wonderful times, Lizzie later spoke of them with great feeling. It was many years since her spirit filled experience with God, she was unable to talk to anyone about it, most of the people she knew did not speak her language, and were not aware of her heavenly salvation.

The farm remained unsold, Lizzie began to worry about her son not being able to pursue his own life and career. She decided it was time for him to go to England with his two younger siblings, Marie Louise and Alston. Together they would be able to send home financial help for the younger ones and prepare a home for them on their arrival in Britain, when ever that might be.

It was the beginning of nineteen fifty two. After a period of mourning, the British people were preparing for the coronation of Queen Elizabeth 11. Beatson was determined to witness, first hand, this memorable occasion. He took up his position some two or three days before the great day, equipped with overnight protection, waterproof cover, survival rations and a note pad and pen. His ability and prowess as a writer came to the fore during this period. He noted in intimate detail, the crowds of people, children and old people, men and women of all ages ,nationalities, colour and creeds, gathering together to see Her Majesty passing by in front of them.

He noted the elaborate decorations of the streets, the lamp posts, the trees, the buildings giving a hugely festive air to the chattering crowds. He noted in detail the costumes and uniforms of the attendant guards, the carriages, and the finery of foreign dignitaries and relations of the Royal British house hold. He noted the robes worn by the young and beautiful Queen as she passed before him. He was unable to describe the delight of the roaring crowds when they finally saw her, being swept along with the excitement of the whole dramatic, memorable occasion.

It was very exciting, and very, very different to anything he had ever experienced before, he figured no amount of radio coverage could report the detail of the event and he was determined that Lizzie would get a share of it on the farm. Some days later a roll of papers arrived from England, several newspapers and a sheaf of pages that Beatson had written during the days he spent in the crowds of on lookers. After reading this interesting account Lizzie circulated the report to many of her interested Indian friends and to the American Doctor who still served his time in Damoh.

In Britain, masses of people were purchasing their very first television sets to see for themselves the great event. If perchance you were unable to afford a television set, many households grouped together in the home that could afford one.

Queen Elizabeth had made her vows to serve the people of Britain and the nations of the Empire for the rest of her life. The days of the coronation made a huge impression on Beatson, he was very British in his outlook and cherished the privilege he had of being in London for this event.

Beatson soon joined a Church in Brixton, their beliefs were to observe the seventh day Sabbath as written in the law of God. Keep the Sabbath day to sanctify it, as the Lord thy God hath commanded thee. Six days thou shalt labour, and do all thy work: but the seventh day is the Sabbath of the Lord thy God.

Attending the same Church , was a young German girl, who worked in England. She was on a short twelve month working permit in an effort to learn the English language. She had decided to leave war ravaged Germany where memories of Hitler's regime still remained fresh in her mind. Because her family worshipped on the Sabbath, they were suspected of being Jews and during the war years feared persecution from the Nazis.

She could clearly remember having to stand for hours on end in line with thousands of other youngsters with her right hand raised in salute to Hitler. If perchance the arm would drop a fraction, the older child in the line behind would prod her sharply where upon her arm would go up again.

She remembers clearly the shelling and the bomb blasts that started the damage to her ear drums causing her in later life to become totally deaf. She remembered the day Nazis officials called at her home, she was eleven years old .They demanded right of entry to the house, the girl stood with her little arms on the door posts, refusing them entry past her., insisting there was no one in the house. She had told her beautiful blonde mother to stay hidden indoors. She had heard of rapes and attacks of young women who subsequently bore the perfect Arian race that Hitler craved, a race of fair skinned, blonde, blue eyed people. The Nazis soldiers retreated.

Beatson, who was totally absorbed in The Word of God, would visit Speakers Corner in Hyde Park London, most Sabbath afternoons, and taking up his position on the soap box would courageously expound God's Word. It was the recreational pass time for many people to heckle the speaker, interrupting and mocking him, so trying to stop who ever it was from continuing with their speeches. Beatson could take any one on without losing his confidence. His sister Flame would often accompany him and sing a song of praise, which held most of the audience in rapt attention.

The young German girl, whose name was Ingebourg also went to listen. She was falling in love with the Anglo Indian speaker. He was so good looking and his knowledge of the Scriptures made her admiration of him go further than skin deep. It was nineteen fifty five, her twelve month work permit was running out, and she was to return to Germany in a week or so. Beatson was informed about this and almost as if he awoke from a dream, he realised he was attracted to the young woman.

He panicked, would she ever return to England, would he ever see her again. After service that sabbath morning, he invited her home to meet Lizzie and the other members of the family. He hadn't even mentioned her before now. Lizzie was delighted by this down to earth, no nonsense young lady. "When are you going to marry my son?" Lizzie asked.. Inge almost choked, "marry her son, why this was the first time she'd been out with him, and worse than that, the first time he'd even noticed her." They spent that Sabbath together.

Beatson invited her out on the Sunday, "Lets go for a cycle ride" he said. She told him that she was returning to Germany on the Wednesday of that week. I'll take the day off tomorrow" he said, "We'll spend some time together". It was a lovely Monday. "Will you come back to England?" he asked.

"I don't know, I'd like to, but I really don't know." He took the Tuesday off work, since it was the last full day she'd be in England. On Tuesday, he took her in his arms and kissed her, "Will you marry me?" he asked.

Inge has been often heard to say, she would have left every thing, her mother, her brothers, sisters, her home and her country, to be with this man. She would have gone round the world, crossed every sea, climbed every mountain, done almost anything to be his wife. She loved him so dearly. For twelve months, she'd dreamed of this, never for a moment expecting it would really happen. "Yes", she whispered, "Yes, I will marry you."

On Wednesday he went to the station to kiss her goodbye. After a brief visit at Christmas, Beatson and Inge arranged their wedding for August the following year.

Now consider the situation. Germany and many of its inhabitants were influenced by the colour prejudice of Hitler's regime Jews, gypsies, coloured people, blacks and disabled people had been butchered by the million, there was no place for Moslems, Hindus, or people with Asian backgrounds. Oh yes, the war was over, but try as they might the legacy of the Hitler regime was still evident. In decades to come, attitudes might change and people of all colours and religions might be accepted to a point.

Beatson was asked to speak at Inge's home Church that Christmas in nineteen fifty five, the translation of his sermon given by his young fiancée. He was received with surprise, how could a man with a brown face know so much about the Bible. How could an Indian, for that is what they thought he was, how could an Indian be so eloquent, so outstandingly good looking. Had he seduced their fair young maiden? The few days he spent with them over that first Christmas proved to them that his intentions were honourable, and unconsciously that his character was exemplary, and the love for the girl was going to last a life time.

They did not see each other until the day before they were married in August nineteen fifty six. Beatson returned from his honeymoon to attend Amela and Rex's wedding. As the male head of the household, he was to give Amela away. They b often practised walking up the aisle, laughing and joking most of the time. "Lets do the German goose step," he'd say. Can you imagine the two of them, strutting through the house, left, right, left right, and raising their feet straight out in front of them like the German soldiers used to do.

The day of Amela's wedding arrived. She stood at the back of the Church, hanging onto Beatson's arm. As the music began to play, Rex turned around to see his lovely bride coming up the aisle to him, he smiled nervously. Beatson squeezed Amela's arm, "Lets do the German goose step," he said. Amela immediately forgot her nerves and almost burst out laughing. "Shush", she whispered, and they continued walking in a slow and dignified manner, smiling as she thought of Beatson's suggestion and their practise walks at home.

Amela forgot her nervousness, it was a simple wedding, there were no bridesmaids, no make up, no lipstick, no expensive wedding ring, no new dress, just the wedding gown that Marie Louise her sister had lent her. But this is Beatson's chapter.

Inge and Beatson went on to have four children. God was the centre of his life. His family, his music, studying the good book, were his main interests. He practised what he preached. He loved God first, he honoured his parents, taking care of Lizzie until the day she died. He kept the Sabbath day holy, he did not lie, steal, cheat, nor covet any material thing.

He taught his children music, and brought them up in the fear and admonition of the Lord. They were truly a lovely family, always keeping in touch with their cousins, sisters, aunts and uncles. Inge gave her life over to being his mate, dedicating her self to caring for his children, and the home and supporting Beatson in his study and writings about the Holy Scriptures.

Their growing children soon joined their parents in performing gospel concerts in Churches, retirement homes, religious conferences, and countless other venues. Beatson wrote his own words and music. His children became proficient musicians, playing the violin, mandolin, piano and guitar, Inge accompanied them all in singing. It was a wonderful sound, they were a wonderful family.

It was now nineteen eighty. Amela had sent invitations to him and his family to attend three days of festivities. Ruth May would be arriving from Australia to meet her long separated siblings and the families they had produced. Would they ever stop talking, singing and laughing together, would they, or could they talk of anything else but their childhood and the memories of the Raj.

Marie Louise An American Memory.

Little can be written about Marie Louise. After her emigration to England, she joined the British Army, where social engagements often meant meeting up with American G.Is and Airmen. She joined the ball room dance class and met an American Airman called Bill. After a passionate courtship she married Bill. Marie Louise was a very beautiful young woman, she inherited the figure of her mother Lizzie, with a full bosom, tiny waist and slender hips and thighs. Her eyes were the colour of deep amber, and her trendy hairstyle and dress sense could have passed her off as a film star.

Bill and Marie Louise had four children, sadly the first son developed multiple sclerosis and was confined to a wheel chair until his early death at the age of twenty four. Marie Louise . She carried him about every where, lifting him on and off the school bus. The authorities would then furnish him with another wheel chair and he would be pushed through the school doors into which ever class room he had to attend. She was devastated by his death. It was at about this time her marriage to Bill began to decline.

Marie Louise lost touch with the English Anglo Indians after her divorce from Bill. She thought they would sit in judgement over her for this un Christian act, little realizing divorces were taking places all over the world including amongst her own family.

During a visit to the States, Alston and Amela met her three other children. Kimberly, Billy and Robyn. Amela remembers how Billy cried when he saw his Aunt. Her mannerisms, the arm movements, the way she reclined in an arm chair, the phrases she used, things that reminded him of his mother. Things that would not be recognised as similar, if Marie Louse had still been alive.

Amela had not seen her sister since the day after her wedding to Rex. She had returned the wedding dress and train she borrowed from Marie Louise, and went on to her honeymoon, Marie Louise went to America that week and never saw the family again.

She died at the age of fifty eight, Amela had lost touch with the children for years before the nineteen eighty re-union, and was there fore unable to send them an invitation to the farm in the Pennines. After the death of Marie Louise, her daughter Kimberly found letters and addresses in the attic of her mother's home and was able to trace the English family again. Trans Atlantic visits took place, the cousins meeting each other for the first time.

Marie Louise is always remembered as the young and lovely girl they last saw decades before. Her life in America took her away from the family and the re-unions. A white wisteria is planted in Amela's French garden in memory of her sister, it reminds her of the gown she wore on her wedding day to Rex.

Alston The Athlete.

Alston was the fifth in line, the brother whose likeness was so obvious on the Dining Room Wall in the Heritage property. How can one carry family genes for four hundred years.? Lizzie loved him very specially, may be that is why he turned out to be such a family orientated man. He recalls vividly the adventure he had with Beatson on the bullock cart, when he was trying to prop Beatson up and seeing the blood gushing out of his brother's leg. He still tells of the screams that could be heard all over the village hospital when the Indian Doctor was sewing up his gashed thigh. It was Alston who could hear the motor bike in the distance, and silently prayed it was Locky "please come and get us", he thought, recalling later that Locky knew nothing of their hunting adventure.

When he had finished his education in Allen, the brother school up in the Himalayas, Alston accompanied by Marie Louise and Beatson came to England.. Lizzie missed them terribly, but she recognised it was best for the future of all three of them to go to England and carve out a future for themselves, in a country where they could be understood, and where they could put their good education to proper use.

Alston took a job in a metal polishing factory where alongside his brother they were able to earn a decent wage and send the surplus home to Lizzie to assist in farm expenses and the lives of the younger ones. Lizzie longed to join them in Britain, but was unable to do so until the legal difficulties were ironed out. The property remained in the name of Gerry, a minor, and each time a prospective buyer turned up, he'd back out of the sale thinking that the farm could be claimed back at any time once Gerry reached the age of majority.

Having reduced the price time and time again, when the farm was finally sold, Lizzie only had sufficient to pay for the cruise liner fares to England and a small deposit for the purchase of a home .

Alston joined the British Army along with his sister Marie Louise. His posting took him to Iraq, where for months he lived under canvas and suffered the intolerable heat. He contracted malaria, a recurring illness that left him weak after each bout. On his return to the British Isles, he was posted some forty miles north of Aberdeen in Scotland to a place called Peterhead.

One Sunday afternoon, a group of army lads went down to the beach to play a game of football. At the same time a group of giggly girls were on the beach, they were eyeing the lads up and down. Alston turned to check out the beauties. One girl stood out from the crowd. She was tall and fair haired, she had the figure of a model, slender and athletic. He couldn't take his eyes off her, hang the football, he could play that any time he liked. The girl saw him looking and smiled at him.

One enchanted daytime, when he saw this stranger, across a crowded beach, oh he knew, yes he knew, he'd have her one day. Today he had found her, and he'd never, never let her go. He did not know her name, her address, her phone number or her nationality, but in the words of the song, "Once he had found her, he'd never, never let her go."

He smiled at her , left the game of football and strolled over to her. "Hi", he said, "My name is Alston, my friends call me AL, whats yours." "Rea," she replied, "I saw you looking at me when you were playing football, aren't you going to finish your game? " "No, " said Al, "I'll walk you home if you're staying in the town." She spoke with a broad Scottish accent. Her heart beat excitedly , "He looks like Elvis Presley" she thought, "the best looking boy on the beach." It was a lovely warm day in Aberdeen, not usual for the time of year. She noticed he was more sun tanned than the rest of the lads, probably due to his service in Iraq. As the weeks went by they saw each other on every occasion. She did not understand when he explained to her that he was an Anglo Indian.

"What ever is an Anglo Indian, ?" she thought. Rea found herself day dreaming about Alston. She mentioned him to her mother, "What does he look like", the mother wanted to know. "Like Elvis Presley, I'll bring him home one day, if he wants to come."

Her Scottish father grunted his disapproval, "Elvis Presley, don't like him much, that hip swinging suggestive singer, I don't want you to have any thing more to do with that fellow," he said.

When Rea took him home, her parents were very polite, Alston sensed their disapproval. Rea was only seventeen years old, Alston but twenty one. His passion for her raged, could think of nothing else but the sylph like goddess, he wanted to posses her, now and forever. He asked permission to marry her. "No," said her father, "She is much too young, in any case I don't want her to marry you, an Anglo Indian, or what ever you call yourself." The parents categorically refused consent.

Rea got a form from the Registry Office and asked her friend to forge her mother's signature. Alston took the form to the Registry Office and fixed a date for the wedding. Rea and Alston told nobody about this, the only person who knew was the friend who had signed the document. On the morning of the wedding, suspecting there might be trouble, Rea dressed in a short cotton skirt, a plain cotton tee shirt and rope soled sandals. She quietly opened her bedroom window and climbed out, she had no money, no handbag, no make up, nothing but the clothes she stood up in.

She ran as fast as she could to the Registry Office. Alston was waiting there for her. Together they ran into the Registry Office and the Registrar bolted the door behind them. A couple who were arranging their own wedding date, was called in to be their witnesses. They did not know who they were. and never ever saw them again.

The ceremony began, "Do you take this woman to be your lawfully wedded wife", "I do." said Al, "hurry, hurry " he thought. The Registrar continued, "Do you take this man to be your lawfully wedded husband" "I do," Rea felt like repeating it a hundred thousand times. "I do, I do, please get on with it" she thought.

"By the power that is vested in me" the Registrar continued, "Hurry up, please hurry up, never mind the power". "I now pronounce you man and wife, you may kiss your bride" Al could have cried, he swept her off her sandaled feet and kissed her as if he could not bear to let her go, even for a second.

Suddenly there was a hammering on the Registry door, the young newly weds looked scared, they knew who it was, they clung onto each other. The Registrar walked slowly to the locked door, "Wait a moment," he tried to be as polite as he possibly could be. He returned to the table, "Sign here please," he said to Alston and Rea, then he invited the witnesses to add their signature to the certificate.

The hammering went on, louder and longer. There was confusion outside in the corridor, some one was trying to silence the person who was hammering on the door. Rea knew who it would be. "Open the door," said the hammerer. "You have my daughter in there."

Rea's mother burst in, "come home at once", she yelled. The Registrar put his hand on her arm and quietly told her to leave the room. "I will not go without my daughter," she screamed.

"She is married now, and can go wherever she likes with her new husband. Rea's mother burst into tears, tears of anger and frustration.

"Never you come into my house again," said her mother, "I never want to see you again," and she stormed out of the office.

Alston had a ticket to London in his pocket along with a five pound note. He held her hand and smiled into her beautiful eyes, clouded with tears of relief, of fear and of pain. "Come on darling," he said, "We'll go down to London and see my Mum, and my family, they're going to love you."

Just how he wangled her ticket to London, no one can remember, sufficient to say, they boarded the train at Aberdeen and found two seats in a secluded corner of a carriage. Alston could not let her go, the ring which was on her finger had come from Woolworth's, bought for a few shillings, but signified a union which would last a lifetime

He kissed her again and again, "No more AL, " she said, "Not here, people will be boarding this train." They arrived in London after the most delightful journey you could imagine. The day was beautiful, the scenery magnificent and their wonderful world filled with love. They did not notice the changing weather as they journeyed through the Lake district of Westmoreland, or the midlands of England, they only knew if this dream journey could go on forever, they would treasure every moment of it.

Amela held a small baby in her arms. She went to open the door when she heard knocking. She embraced her brother and the gorgeous Scottish creature beside him. Amela noticed her slender legs and her tight fitted short skirt, her pretty feet in open toed sandals. "Surely she didn't get married in that ," Amela thought. Rea was nervous to meet Alston's family. Lizzie looked so different from her own mother. She welcomed her beloved son with outstretched arms and hugs and kisses. She eyed Rea up and down, she could see the reason why Alston was attracted to her. The girl was tall with light brown hair and a beautiful figure, she put her arms around Rea and welcomed her into the family.

Amela could barely understand her new sister-in-law, but that did not matter. Alston was so in love with her and now she was a member, a precious member of the family. "She's a Loughran," Amela thought, "And I am not."

Years went by, Alston never failed to keep in touch with his family, he missed Ruth May and Marie Louise and looked forward to seeing them again. He tried to find Marie Louise who had left for America in nineteen fifty six, contacting a number of agencies, all proving to be fruitless.

Alston became a superb athlete, excelling in the game of squash and winning trophy after trophy, in standard competitions and also in the geriatric league. He became a squash instructor, despite the fact that his ankles were causing him pain as he twisted and turned on them in the squash courts.

Now it was nineteen eighty. He had received the invitation from Amela and Rex, informed their children about it and prepared to drive up to Yorkshire. They took two of their kids with them, but the middle one, who had spent weeks converting a van into a state of the art caravanette, drove himself and his young girl friend up in style.

Alston could not wait to arrive at Amela's farm in the Pennines. Here he would re-unite with the rest of his family, the British family of Anglo Indians. Undoubtedly the Guest of Honour would be their big sister Ruth May who was coming from Australia for the first time. It was difficult to describe his jubilation when he saw Ruth May. This promised to be the great family re-union where they could share the almost forgotten memories of the Raj

Flame Reflected in Skye.

Flame was sixth in line, born in a town called Yeotmal in the Central Province of India. She was especially gifted in looks and voice. She had short black hair curling softly around her pretty face, giving her the appearance of a doll. She was about five feet five inches tall, with a dainty bone structure. Flame arrived in England just a few months before Lizzie and the two youngest kids. Lizzie was reluctant to let her go, but since Locky's sister was to accompany her, all would be well. The servants gave her the most amazing send off at Jubulpur, garlands of flowers were ceremoniously hung about her neck. Farewell photos were taken for the family album. Flame was wearing her best suit, home made by the dhurzi, in Damoh. She was wearing a pair of ankle socks, inside her flat black shoes. She looked like a simple country lass, and as old fashioned as ever.

Flame was afraid of Locky during his life time, Lizzie, who was conscious of this, favoured Flame above her other sisters. She was a very good athlete, but more than this she was a lovely singer and an elocutionist. When on stage she was very dramatic, no poem was ever the same after Flame had learnt to recite it. She kept the school audiences spell bound every time she started to entertain.

Her sister Amela was a very tall girl, seventh in line and only two years younger than Flame. By and large the two sisters got on very well, they played together a lot during the holidays and squabbled a lot during the school term.. The school did not allow fighting to go on amongst the pupils, but behind the staff backs, much of it did continue. One day the two sisters were squabbling, Amela bit her sister on the hand, so hard that it began to bleed.

A member of staff saw Flame trying to stop her hand from bleeding and keeping a handkerchief tied around it drew attention to what she might have been hiding. The teacher told Flame to go down to the tiny school hospital situated behind the dining room and servants quarters. When Sister Young saw the wound, she asked Flame who bit her. "Nobody, Miss" the girl said, "I fell down the steps near the Cambridge block and caught my hand on the railing. Of course this was a lie, had Sister Young found out it was Amela who had bitten her , she would have been beaten within an inch of her life. Flame knew this, and to protect her sister she told a bare faced lie.

Flame was darker in complexion than the rest of her family, it was most becoming, but in Anglo Indian India and indeed in the British Raj, the darker you were, the less looked up to, you were. One wonders if this inherent colour consciousness was in Locky. He rarely spoke to Flame, she could remember running and hiding under the beds when ever she heard his footsteps in the house. Her curly hair would get caught in the springs of the bed, causing her to cry, this would only make him angry with her, and he would start yelling.

On her arrival in England Flame blossomed into a beautiful young lady. She took a job in a large bank in central London, she felt was the most wonderful city in the world. She was away from the protective eye of her mother, and the fashion restrictions she knew in India. London, the capital of the British Empire., allowed her to expand and do her own thing.

Every one fell in love with Flame, not only for her good looks but for her warm and caring personality. Gone was the scared little girl, gone was the teenager who lacked confidence, gone were the bobby socks and the flat black lace up shoes, every day saw her grow in confidence. She grew in stature with her associates and banking colleagues, . Many young men asked for dates, which she demurely declined.

The farm in India was finally sold, Gerry and Amela were coming to Britain with Lizzie. The liner Stratheden was due to dock at Tilbury, the passengers would then transfer to a train that would carry them to central London. Flame could not wait to see them, she dressed herself in fashionable clothes, put make up on her cute face, wore the highest shoes that showed off her dainty legs and went to Tilbury to meet Lizzie, Gerry and Amela.

The war which had started fifteen years to the date before, was finally over and won some seven years later. The newspapers of the day still carried reminders of the announcement by Winston Churchill, tales of events and the involvement of the public. It was Amela's birthday the next day, she would be sixteen. Flame was standing by a newspaper man's stall reading the headlines. Amela was one when war was declared, she waited for the disembarkation of the passengers. Lizzie and the children almost walked past her, not recognising this fashion plate as one of the family.

"Mum", Flame shouted, Lizzie turned back and Flame ran into her mother's arms, "Mum, Gerry, Amela, welcome to England", she was almost crying with excitement as were the other three. "England is a wonderful place with wonderful people." Lizzie could not let Flame go, she held her hand as if she were a little girl again. "I want to be the first to show you the things I have seen and learned to love in the few months I have been here." Flame looked so different, where was the timid little girl with bobby socks and flat shoes, with a gathered skirt and a button through blouse? "You look so beautiful darling," Lizzie kissed her again.

Flame was so proud to show Lizzie the British way of transport, we'll catch the train from this station Mum, we'll then catch the tube to Aunty Florence's place in Morden, don't worry, I'll take you there, don't be scared."

Amela and Gerry were dumb founded. They could not stop looking at every little detail of their new adventure, the roads, the buses, the trains, the scenery. Wonderful England, where every thing was quiet, clean and organised, we're here at last, could this be true, could this really be happening to them.

They arrived in Morden, they were welcomed into the home of Florence, Lizzie's sister. On the dining room wall, was a shelf with a square looking contraption sitting on it, a wooden box with a moving picture. "What do you think of television Amela? Flame asked. Amela who was enchanted by every thing she had seen so far, was totally unimpressed by the television. What was so great about television. A bell started ringing in the other room, someone picked up a telephone handset and started speaking to Steele who was still in India. Now this was impressive. Five thousand miles away in India, and he could speak to his beloved mother who had only just arrived in England.

Amela never failed to be impressed by the telephone, even fifty years later, one could press buttons on a hand set and speak to any one in the world. How many people are there in the world, more than six thousand billion, it never failed to be a source of wonder, the lovely voice of your son, your daughter, your lover or your mother. Unique, each one unique and as easily definable as one's face, thank heaven for satellite communication.

Flame very soon began dating boys. Lizzie would be introduced to them, and would either give her consent or not. Each time Flame would listen to her mother and take her advice. "Bring them to Church with us", Lizzie would say. Of course this frightened many of the suitors away, never to be seen again.

On her way to work each morning, she noticed a very good looking English man looking at her. Each day he'd smile until one day he plucked up the courage to say "Hello." This went on for several weeks. Flame found herself looking forward to seeing the man and wished he would stop and talk to her. He must have sensed her invitation and did just that. "Come out with me on Sunday", he said, "We can catch the tube to central London and I will show you some of the famous sights."

"I cant do that," she replied, "I go to Church on Sunday, why don't you come with me and meet my mother, my brother, and my sister." Although Peter was a little taken aback by this invitation, never having been a church goer himself, he said he'd love to.

On Sunday, Flame put on her very best dress, high heeled shoes and rouge and lipstick, she couldn't wait to meet Peter outside the little tiny Church Hall in South Wimbledon. .Sure enough, at five minutes to eleven she jumped off the bus and crossed the road. Peter was waiting there, he was very fashionably although unusually dressed. He wore a black suit with a velvet collar, the suit jacket reached down to his knees, and his matching trousers fitted tightly down to his ankles. His tie was no thicker than a boot lace which held together the collar of his immaculately white shirt.

Flame's heart jumped, what a good looking man, could this be the man she met on the way to work each morning. "Mum," Flame said, "I'd like you to meet Peter." Lizzie had been told about Peter, she shook his hand and said , "I'm so glad to meet you Peter, and to know you attend Church. "Peter swallowed hard, he had no idea what went on in a Pentecostal Church like this. There were no pews, no stained glass windows, no statues of Christ or the Virgin Mary. Lizzie eyed him up and down, being fashionable herself, leading rather than following trends, she thought he looked very suitable.

Peter was enchanted by every thing, most of all by this dark haired, dark eyed girl who stood beside him. The Pastor of the Church eyed Peter up and down disapprovingly, he recognised that the fashion he was wearing was associated with unruly youth of the day called Teddy Boys, they had received bad press and all of them were tarred with the same brush.

After a few weeks, during which time Peter attended Church on Sundays and during the week to Bible Studies, he felt he'd had enough and stopped. The Pastor reprimanded Lizzie for encouraging Peter in his courtship with Flame, not only that but he objected strongly about the way Flame was dressed. "I don't think she should paint her face with rouge and lipstick," he said, "She looks like a harlot."

Lizzie was pretty shocked by this. She mentioned it to Flame, The Pastor does not want you to attend Church with paint on your face," she said. A huge row ensued. Flame, who by now was in love with Peter and stood up for him and her own morality, told Lizzie she was leaving home. "Peter's parents said I could go and live with them until we are married," she said to her mother.

Amela missed her sister, they were very good friends, often sharing courtship details, laughing and joking when things were mentioned which were unmentionable. Flame was invited to sing at a local youth club. That night Peter decided to escort her. She wore an emerald green dress, her tiny waist pulled in by a wide black belt, her patent leather shoes adding four inches to her height.

Every eye turned to look at her when she made her entrance into the club. Flame was nervous, shaking inside, trying not to let Peter know, trying to show more confidence that she felt.. "Ladies and gentlemen," the compare began to speak, "Please welcome our guest singer this evening, Miss Flame Loughran." The pronunciation of her name made her smile, no one could pronounce it correctly if they saw it written, and no one could spell it correctly if they heard it spoken. She took the microphone from him and waited for the introduction from the band. She looked directly into Peter's eyes.

"Love is a many splendoured thing," she sang in a clear strong voice, *"It's the April rose that only grows in the early spring,*

"Love is natures way of giving, the reason to be living, the golden crown that makes a man a king." The love she felt for Peter inspired her to sing like she never sang before,

"Once on a high and windy plain - she continued,

"Love is a many splendoured thing."

The applause rang out loud and long. "Encore, encore," the audience shouted. She handed the microphone back to the compare and without taking her eyes off Peter she returned to her seat near him He looked deep into her eyes, then taking her hand in his and not saying a word, he lead her out of the club.

They walked into the cool April night, then taking her in his arms he said, "Flame, will you marry me, I love you so much, you are the most beautiful girl I have ever seen, and I want you to be my wife." She stood still in the circle of his arms, her heart beating like a drum. Yes of course she would marry him, but first of all she would have to obtain consent from Lizzie. She said, "What will your parents say if you were to marry an Anglo Indian girl, people in this country are prejudiced against colour, they might say they are not, but if their son or daughter marries someone from India or the Caribbean , it's a different story, however much they claim to be unprejudiced.

"Listen Flame," Peter said, when I was in the merchant navy, I met many girls from Hong Kong and Singapore, I remember writing home to my brother and telling him I'd never marry an English girl, now that is not the reason I want to marry you, I love you and want to marry you for no other reason." "Oh Peter, she started to cry, "Suppose my mother does not give her consent," "I'll wait for you till you are old enough not to need consent, it will only be two years, my darling."

Lizzie gave her consent. They were married in a Registry Office because the Pastor of the Church would not conduct a wedding between a Teddy Boy and a girl who wore rouge and lipstick. Flame's dress was made of organza, mid calf length, she wore high heeled white shoes and a large brimmed white hat. She looked stunning.

Peter was unlike Rex. He was full of charm and communication, a vivacious character who worked in various clubs and gambling houses as a croupier. Flame accompanied him to work until she fell pregnant with their first child. Steven was born about eighteen months after they were married, he was a beautiful child with dark eyes that danced when you looked at him. A few years later Flame gave birth to a second son , whom she named Paul. Flame idolised her two sons, giving them what ever they wanted and that she could afford. It was at about this time the marriage to Peter began to fail. Just what happened to cause the break down nobody quite knows, they began to live separate lives. Both were devastated by the split, but as is so typical of youth, they were unable to discuss their problems and work them out.

Lizzie had died years before, Flame found comfort in the arms of Peter's friend Jim. A few years later she married Jim and seemed very happy. Her home and garden were her number one priorities. Somehow she managed to get through this crisis in her life without sharing her burden with Amela.

Now it is nineteen eighty. Amela had sent her the invitation to attend the welcome re-union for their big sister Ruth May. "I'll do the cooking," she said, "I'll bring two or three different curries in stainless steel buckets, I'll cook the rice and the parathas when I am at your farm, leave it to me," she said. So Amela did.

Amela Gifted and Grateful

Amela was the seventh of the eight Loughran children. Lizzie had given birth first to a boy, then a girl, a boy a girl, a boy, a girl, then breaking the pattern, Amela is born before Gerry. Is this the reason why she is blessed and gifted, could seven be a lucky number.

Wynberg Allen, the school the children attended was set way up in the foothills of the Himalayas. It was founded in the late nineteenth century. The objective was to provide for and give children of wholly or partly European descent, an education based on Protestant Christian Principals, to maintain such children and to give them an academic and practical training conducive to economic welfare and happiness.

Amela was grateful to Gerald Smith and her great aunt Marie Baker for depositing a very large sum of money into the Society funds to provide and pay for the education of all Locky's children. They did not know that Locky would go on to father eight children. The school term started each year in the beginning of March and continued non stop till the end of November. During the month of July there was a short mid term break when a few of the scholars would go home, that is if their home was less than a days journey away from Wynberg Allen. The Loughran children would not go home because their journey each way took three days.

The staff would endeavour to make this week as entertaining as possible for the kids that remained behind. They would organise entertainment, a visit to the skating rink, the cinema, a walk in the khuds, and valleys. The ramble in the valleys was hated, due to the leeches which could work their way into the clothes and undergarments of the children and suck their blood. Screams would often be heard at night when the kids were undressing, a leech could have inched its way up to ones collar or into ones knickers, not being detected until the garments were removed.

At the end of each year, an exam was set to all classes, if you passed this examination you were then permitted to promote to the next standard. However, if you failed, you would have to remain in the same standard until such time as you passed. It did not matter if it took two or five years, you would not have been promoted. When Amela was thirteen years old, she was in the same class as a girl who was nineteen. The head mistress kindly requested the parents of the girl to remove her from school as no amount of teaching, private or otherwise would enable her to proceed to a higher class.

The customs and traditions of the school were based on the British private education system, principals were rigid and founded on Christian teachings.

The girl's school was set on the tops of two adjacent hills in the town of Mussoorie . The main building, which housed the Assembly Hall and the Dining Room, was an imposing structure which looked like a huge ship. The senior girl's dormitories were surrounded by an open, low walled veranda and built above the main halls. They were fronted by an apartment which was the private domain of the Head Mistress. From her vantage point she was able to observe the carrying on of the pupils almost where ever they were in the grounds.

The dining hall stood behind the Assembly Hall. A huge place with four long tables set side by side down its length . Benches were set along side the tables to seat the two hundred or so scholars. At one corner of the room, set to one side, was a small table lavishly laid for the member of staff who would be over seeing meal times. On the wall opposite the large entrance door way , were four framed photographs of serious looking British people. They were the Founders of the school, named Allen, Foy, Powell and West. The tables were named after the Founders, and students were allocated different tables. Amela and Flame were both in West House.

Founders Day was the main event in the school calendar. On or around the nearest convenient day to October the eighth each year, the whole atmosphere of the austere school changed. It was more exciting than Christmas day to the kids. You were awakened by a happy, humorous Dormitory Matron, and encouraged to prepare yourself for breakfast wearing your best school uniform and polished black shoes.

When the school gong was heard you went downstairs and lined up in the correct house lines. West House was last in to the Dining Room. The entire school remained standing behind the benches until the grace was said. "For what we are about to receive, may the Lord make us truly thankful, Amen." The shuffling around was quite something when the kids all hastened to sit down and eat the cold porridge or the cold dhal which was set out on alternate days. The three slices of bread, one scraped with margarine using a feather, another with a scraping of jam, and the third one dry, was set out for each child.

The girl at the head of each table would pour out the tea for the students nearest her. One day Marie Louise remembered doing this and finding a dead frog at the bottom of the jug. However this did not happen today, it was Founders Day. After breakfast, the girls stood behind their benches and said grace again, this time, "For what we have received may the Lord make us truly thankful, Amen."

The school gong sounded and the girls were again lined up to take their place in the Assembly Hall for the thanksgiving service. The Scholars from the brother school Allen marched up the hill to the joint service. At the platform to the left of the stage, was a four tiered cake decorated in green and gold icing, so beautiful, it out classed any wedding cake you ever did see. During the service the head girl and boy cut the cake which was later distributed to students and staff.

The Principal, School Heads and Staff Members sat on the stage. The uniformed students, boys to the left of the aisle and girls to the right stood before their benches awaiting the welcome and greeting from the Principal.

The Principal rose to his feet and greeted everyone. He stood proudly clutching the sides of his gown. Hymn after hymn was sung and the Scriptures were read, a short speech preceded the presentation of special awards which were the high light of the Service.

"Amela Loughran," her name was called, she was not paying attention and failed to recognise what was going on. "Amela Loughran," the girl at the side of her nudged her sharply. "You're being called up to the platform." She rose to her feet and hastened to the stage, "For outstanding performance in the class room and on the sports field you are presented with the School Colours.

This was an honour never to be forgotten. Only six girls received the colours that year, most students left school after their entire education never having received this honour. Amela was dumb founded, gifted and grateful. After the ceremony, the boys returned to their own school, and the girls changed into their sports kit and followed in line down the steep hill to Allen, where the track events and relay races were going to beheld. The event was very formal. The high ranking staff and visitors were seated on the grand stand and awaited the march past..

Each house was lead by its captain, and two banner bearers. The procession came on to the sports field, house by house. As they marched past to the accompaniment of the band, the captain of each house gave the command. "West House, eyes right," at which point the banner bearers lowered their banner and the students wearing their matching kit and sporting rosettes in the house colour, looked to the grand stand whilst continuing the march past.

Flame and Amela carried the banner for West House. The motto of which was "Nil des perandum." Never despair. They say, "School days are golden days," the children were not aware of this until much later in life, when the teachings and principals they learnt never forsook them.

At the end of the day of activity on the sports field, came the presentation of the trophies. It was an opportune time when the girls could look at the boys and giggle at their handsome faces and fine physiques, the girls then returned to their own school in preparation for the big feast. After returning to their dormitories and donning their best "mufti", they lined up at the sound of the gong, awaiting entrance in to the dining hall.

It looked like a different place. The four long tables were set with spotlessly white linen clothes and laid with china and cutlery the students had never seen before. Flowers and decorations adorned each table An extra table was set at the top end of the Dining Room for the staff members. It was no more special than the tables for the students. The smell that permeated from the kitchens was mouth watering.

Grace was said. The bearers came with huge trays piled high with delicious pilau and large dishes of chicken curry. They could have as many helpings as they wished, the whole lot washed down with glasses of orange juice. What a fabulous feast. The austere looking photographs of the founders that graced the dining room wall almost looked as if they were smiling at the happiness of the children as they munched their way through the meal. When the first course was cleared away, large trays full of gelabies were put on the table. Gelabies are an Indian sweet made with flour, deep fried and soaked in hot sugar syrup and served in little coils. A perfect compliment to the curry and rice of the main meal.

Amela never forgot that day, firstly because she had been given her colours and secondly because she had been presented with a trophy for winning the four relay race. It had been a wonderful year.

There were only eight children in her class. All of who were going to sit their Cambridge Examinations in early December when the rest of the school had left to go to their homes. Amela however, was not going to sit the Junior Cambridge Exams, she had decided to give it a miss and go for the Senior Exam the following year. The standard eight teachers had agreed that she was clever enough to do that. The other students in her class would have to take a further two years to sit their final standard ten, senior Cambridge Exam.

Amela had not really been serious about her studies that year. She was confident that she'd pass her October Tests, after which she gave all her text books to her colleagues, and sold her exercise books to the bunya for a few annas with which she purchased a small bag of jigs and sugary jag.

It was Friday, the thirteenth of November nineteen fifty three.

"The head Mistress wants to see you in her office Amela," her class teacher told her. She went up into the private domain of the head mistress, a place which she had never seen before. She was scared, what had she done? Had the head mistress found out that she had sold her exercise books to the bunya.? She had an excuse ready to answer if this was the case. "You see Miss, my class work is finished, I will be going home with the rest of the school in two weeks time."

"What would you do if I told you, you had to sit your Junior Cambridge Exam Amela?" "I'd mug like mad Miss," Amela answered.

"Well, there has been a mistake at the start of the year. We submitted a list of applications into the University of Cambridge, your name was sent and your roll number has arrived today, I'm afraid you will have to sit the exams. I know this comes as a complete shock and surprise to you , but do the best you can, I'm confident you will be able to manage it."

Amela ran downstairs and gave her classmates her terrible news. She tried to collect text books, but found only those with pages torn from them. Her exercise books were ripped up for wrapping paper at the bunyas. She tried to mug and revise with nothing but her memory to fall back on.

The rest of the school went home, including Flame and Gerry. She felt alone and scared. Lizzie would kill her if she failed this exam. She had messed about all year long, telling herself it did not matter, since she was going to sit her Seniors next year. The night before each exam that December, she would sit up late in the senior girls toilets trying to read some of the tatty text books. The two weeks passed quickly. Only three girls were taking their senior exams that year and eight doing the Juniors. In other schools up and down the country, thousands of pupils were sitting the exams on the same days and at the same times.

They went home after this eventful two weeks. The results were not due till April next year. Much had happened during the winter months away from school. Flame had left for England, Amela had had a horrendous accident in the March just prior to her expected return to school ,and the farm so unexpectedly had been sold. Lizzie, Amela and Gerry were at their grandmother's house in Jubulpur awaiting the departure of their cruise liner which would take them to England.

The post man arrived. Amela took the letters from him and noticed one which bore the diagonal lines in gold and green which signified a letter was from her school. She knew they would be the results of her Cambridge Exam. She took the letters to Lizzie then hastened out of the house to avoid the telling off which she knew she would be getting.

An hour or two later when she arrived home again, hoping that Lizzie would have calmed down, she was met with these words: "Well done darling, I've received your exam results, not only have you passed with flying colours, but you got a distinction in English and have won a scholarship for coming twenty sixth in the whole province." Amela could no believe what she was hearing, she was overjoyed, the scholarship meant that she could complete her education free of charge if she stayed in the same Province. The scholarship was awarded to the forty best students of each Province. Since the farm had been sold , she would not be returning to that school again. Amela did not care if she never went to school again, she was soon to be going to the land of her dreams - ENGLAND.

England was enjoying peace after the second world war. Rationing had stopped and the people had a super abundance of food and housing , in fact it had been said "they never had it so good. The young Queen Elizabeth had been on the throne for about two years. She had given birth to the heir apparent and the nation was enjoying a wonderful period of peace and tranquillity. Migrants were arriving in their droves from the sub Continent and the West Indies taking up occupations in conducting the transport system in major cities and as hospital orderlies all around the country.

Racial prejudice, whilst making head line news in the United States of America, was not evident in Britain. There was an under current of it but individual stories varied from total acceptance to total rejection. The words of an American song rather summed up the underlying atmosphere, "If you're white, your alright, if you're brown, stick around, but if you're black, oh brother, get back, get back, get back."

The Dining Room Wall

Amela arrived in England on her sixteenth birthday. Sweet sixteen, and never been kissed. She was tall and slim with long black hair and a gentle sun tanned complexion. She was full of vitality, enthusiasm and the spirit of adventure. During her very first month in England she went with Lizzie to the youth employment bureau. The clerk in charge gave her three cards bearing the names of three companies who were looking for a young receptionist for their offices. "Take which ever one you please Amela, they will call you for interview and you will be able to commence work as soon as you want to."

In preparation for this life changing experience, Amela bought a pleated grey skirt from a shop called Marks and Spencer, she wore it with a simple white blouse and a cardigan. Lizzie of course accompanied her on this interview. Amela had never been away from home with out the supervision of her mother or a servant, and of course she had never left school without a teacher and her peers being with her.

It is safe to say that Lizzie conducted the interview. After greeting the boss with a simple "Good morning," Amela sat silently, while Lizzie asked the questions.

"What will my daughter be required to do?"

"Who will her boss be?"

"What days will she be working?"

"How many hours a day will she be required to be at the office?"

"Will she be working alone with men?"

"What will her salary be?" etc. etc.

In answer, "Operate the switch board, Mr Gillan, Five days a week from nine till five. No, not alone with men, but there will be men in the adjoining offices, £3 per week."

"Your daughter speaks beautiful English Mrs. Loughran," said the man who was being interviewed, "We would like her to start on Monday next week if that is alright with you."

Amela was surprised, she had hardly said a word, but was very happy that the interview had gone so well and that she was going to start on her very first job. There followed, for the next fifty years questions as to her origin, the land of her birth and her ancestors.

Her complexion was a sun tanned brown, people thought she could have come from India, but was far too tall. She could not have come from the West Indies, her hair was far too straight. She looked as if she might have come from the Mediterranean , Italy, Spain, Turkey, but her English was far too good and her accent far too English. Could it be Ireland with a name like Loughran?

"Let me guess where you come from" was a question which dominated many a conversation for the rest of her life. No one had ever heard of Anglo Indians until Anglo Indians explained it to their associates. Even then it was difficult for people to understand how British they were when they were born in another country. Amela was a typical Anglo Indian, gregarious, welcoming, very easy to communicate with and good looking.

She was installed in the telephone switch board room with an old woman of twenty eight years of age. Sally, worked in her spare time as a sweater model. She showed Amela her port folio of glamour shots of sweaters, tightly pulled over her ample breasts, with the faces of other models super imposed onto her body.

Although Amela regarded Sally as an old woman, she was envious of her figure. Amela didn't even wear a bra, didn't even need one, even at sixteen she was so unlike Flame. She wore no make up, lipstick, or fashionable clothes , and her figure was as flat as a board.

In the meantime, Lizzie too had started work. She would liked to have taken up teaching again. She needed to take a refresher course, but when she saw the lack of discipline in the schools she abandoned that idea. Instead she took the job of a ward orderly in a local hospital. The job was totally beneath her dignity. She often wondered what the servants would say if they saw the Memsahib cleaning toilets or mopping up vomit from the floors. The dhobi would be aghast to see her collecting dirty linen and removing it to the laundry room.

But Lizzie who was a born again Christian, reconciled herself to the job, telling herself that if the Son of God, the creator of the Universe could come to earth and be a carpenter, she would do all the necessary work in His name and for His glory.

Amela was having a wonderful time at work. "Hello Air Pumps," she would say a hundred times a day, then put the caller through to the appropriate office.

Very soon she noticed a tall, handsome, dark haired man going frequently past her office hatch window, on his way to the "Gents" toilet. Even with her lack of experience she was certain he was taking a special interest in her.

"Mum, " she said to Lizzie one day, "There's a man at work, I think he likes me, he keeps passing my window and looking at me."

"He might be looking at Sally," Lizzie said.

"Sally? no Mum, not Sally, she's old, she's twenty eight and has a nose like a parrot." It wasn't till years later that Amela realised that even at twenty eight, a big bust was of interest to most men, thankfully not this one.

"Lend me a bra please Flame," Amela asked her sister one day. "I don't want any one to think I am not grown up."

One day, Flame decided to come to Air Pumps and check out this man. She had heard such glowing reports about him that she couldn't imagine him still chasing Amela when he had seen Flame. In preparation for this nerve wracking encounter, Amela showed Rex a photo of Flame. "I've seen her, " he said. "She is waiting at a bus stop which I cycle past on my way to work each morning."

"Isn't she pretty?" Amela asked Rex, holding her breath while she waited anxiously for his answer.

"Yes, she is," he said, "But she is no where near as pretty as you." Amela was walking on air, no one had ever said that she was prettier than the gorgeous Flame. Each day after that, Amela would go with him into the drawing office and talk to him for the rest of the lunch hour. She showed him photos of her past life in India, he listened in a half hearted manner, not taking his eyes off her for an instant. She listened as he told her of his family, Rex was nineteen years of age and attended a Church youth club. He was taking dancing lessons. She told him of her own family, about Flame, about Gerry and of course about Beatson.

Amela was taking evening classes to learn shorthand and typing. Rex knew the only way to meet her mother Lizzie would be to escort her home after evening class with a hope that Amela would invite him in to meet the family. He also knew she would not go out with him until he had met her mother. Night after night, he walked her to her front door, where she would shake hands with him and say "Good night, I'll see you at work tomorrow Rex."

One evening, she allowed him to hold her hand as they walked home. To her horror, walking in the opposite direction was her brother Beatson, she tried to pull her hand free from Rex's grasp. He, realising she had seen somebody she knew , would not let her hand go.

"Oh hello Rex," Beatson said, "I've heard so much about you, go on in to the house , I wont be a minute and I'll join you there, the rest of the family are indoors."

There was no escaping the inevitable now. Rex went into the house, Flame offered him a cup of coffee , which he did not drink even though she placed the cup in front of him. He had never drunk coffee in his life, not now, nor till the day he died. Gerry, sat on a stool in front of the couple, Lizzie asked him a hundred questions about his family, his job, his prospects and his intentions. Rex was turning redder by the minute. Amela could have died with embarrassment when Gerry threw a newspaper onto the table in front of Rex, he had scribbled on it the words, "Rex came for interview and passed." After an hour of this intense encounter, he said good night to every one and went home. "That's that", Amela thought, "they have frightened him away , he wont want to talk to me again."

Much to her surprise, the next day, he invited her to sit near him at the lunch time canteen visit and to come into the drawing office for their usual chat. She took her place on the high stool in front of his drawing board. They heard some one at the door, Rex went to see who it was trying to push their way in.

It was David who worked with Amela in the switch board room. Rex pushed David in his face and threw him out of the drawing office. then slammed and locked the door. He came back to the drawing board, he lent forward and took her in his gorgeous strong arms .She felt herself shaking in anticipation. She lifted one hand and placed it on his shoulder, then gazing into her beautiful brown eyes, her kissed her softly on her lips.

The world spun out of control. She couldn't see straight, she found it difficult to even breathe normally, her heart pounded like a drum. She had fallen in love with Rex.

Although there were fifteen minutes still to go before lunch time was over, she staggered to her feet. "I'll have to go to the switch board," she said. She could not stand a repetition of this ecstatic moment . She rose to her feet, reeling in her brain. To his eyes, she walked steadily to the door and out of the drawing office. Amela could not concentrate on her work for the rest of the day.

The boss heard of the incident between Rex and David. He called Amela into his office and said she was not to go into the drawing office again. "These two are hot headed teenagers, you are a pretty young girl and completely unaware of the effect you have on them, so to avoid this happening again, please Amela stay away from them during the working hours."

A few weeks after this ecstatic beginning to the romance, Rex invited Amela to a dance which was to be held in the Church Hall for the youth club. She was so excited, she loved dancing, and hoped that Rex was a competent dancer also. She bought a beautiful black taffeta reversible skirt, which flared out into a circle, showing the pink colour of the skirt beneath each time she turned in a dance movement. The gorgeous pink blouse picked out the colour beneath and the whole effect was cinched into a wide black belt which emphasised her small waist.

They caught the bus to South Wimbledon . The lovely rhythmic mid fiftys music welcomed them warmly into the Church Hall. Rex got her a drink of orange juice and asked her to dance. He took her in his strong arms and began twirling her round to the music. She had dreamed of this moment from the time he mentioned taking her to the dance. They had barely begun to dance when she felt her vision blurring, sometimes it was clear, other times partial and sometimes decidedly blurred. She tried at first to avoid this, hoping it would go away and not take its usual course. Experience told her it was an attack of migraine.

Amela first had a migraine attack when she was about nine years old. Nobody had heard of it in school, or at home in India. After reading about it in a woman's magazine in a letter to the Doctor, she realized what it was. No, it was not life threatening, and she was not the only person in the world to suffer from it. Experience told her that it would run its course and she would have to stop what she was doing and go home to bed. After the blurred vision had disappeared, she would get a strange detached sensation in her hand and arm, almost as if it did not belong to her, then a pounding head ache that lasted for hours and only eased when she was sick. She stumbled once or twice losing her balance.

"Rex, I don't feel well, I think I will have to go home". She tried hard to keep the disappointment out of her voice. She thought he would get her coat and escort her to the bus stop for her to go home alone, but he did not.

Lizzie was most surprised to see them come home so early knowing how excited Amela had been to go out with him. "I've got migraine Mum," Amela said, "I have to go to bed." Rex stayed downstairs for a while and then asked Lizzie if he could go up and say good night to his girl friend. Amela had put on a dull beige night dress which opened partly down the front, one that had belonged to Ruth May when she was breast feeding, she then fell into bed awaiting the onslaught of the blinding head ache which she knew would follow.

She thought that Rex would go back to the dance and enjoy the rest of the evening with his friends from the youth club. She felt jealous and tired. She heard a knock on the door and hoped it was him. He quietly walked into the room and knelt down beside the bed. Had she known he would be up she would have taken one of Flame's glamorous night gowns instead of this comfy ugly old thing she was wearing. "How are you feeling Amela?" he whispered. He touched her gently on the head, and tried to kiss the pain away. Before long his mouth found hers and the thrill which she felt over shadowed the pain in her head. He kissed her again and again. She wished that Lizzie was not in the house, then she could lose herself in his arms, but fearing that her mother would also come up to see how she was, Amela kept her ear open.

He started to kiss her neck and found himself undoing the buttons down to her waist. Amela was trembling with excitement, he started touching her breasts and found her protruding nipples. She did not know why she was enjoying this sensation. A strange feeling of pleasure was coming over her body. Rex put his hand under the bedclothes, and began lifting her night dress up to her thighs, she forgot the pain in her head, and endeavoured to stop him raising the night dress any further up her legs. Amela had no idea of what he was trying to do, but subconsciously she knew he must not go any further.

Rex kissed her again and again, he even kissed her soft, young firm breasts. He pulled the covers off her body and wanted to see the mole on her left thigh. "You are the prettiest thing I have ever seen" he said in a hushed breathless voice.

Time flew by, and before long it was ten thirty, the time when Rex had to leave Amela's home. Lizzie shouted up to let him know he had to go. "Amela", he said, "staying with you beats any dance I could have gone to, goodnight my darling", he kissed her one more time and then left the house.

"I want to marry him," she thought before falling to sleep.

Amela was now seventeen years old. Each Saturday Rex would fetch her on his tandem and together they would cycle to a beauty spot in Surrey some twenty five miles away from home. They took drinks and something to eat and spent the entire day swimming in a lake they discovered. Rex taught her to swim. Having come from India and being educated in a boarding school, it was not acceptable for young girls to be seen in a swimsuit . But this was England, and nobody could see her except Rex. Their courtship was getting very exciting, she wanted to be with him more than anyone else, she was seventeen years old, and the Saturday cycle rides were the high light of her week, something she looked forward to with delight.

One fine day they were rolling down a footpath in a place called Leith Hill, the front wheel of the tandem hit a rhododendron root and threw them into a pile of leaves and bracken. Rex pushed the tandem out of the way and edged closer to Amela. He started kissing her, the kisses were given and received with passion. Hidden from the eyes of walkers and ramblers, he began to undo the buttons of her blouse, he lifted her divided skirt out of the way and rolled on top of her.

Then to her surprise, he undid the buttons of his trouser flaps, and took something out which took her breath away. She tried to hide her surprise and shock, she pushed him off her, fastened her blouse buttons and got to her feet. She was shaking, she was scared. He did up his trouser flies, picked up the tandem and continued their cycle ride.

It was May nineteen fifty six. Rex was twenty one years old. It was a beautiful English spring. "Mrs. Loughran, can I get engaged to your daughter please?" Lizzie gave her permission but was horrified when she realized that Rex wanted to marry Amela the week he finished his apprenticeship as a Mechanical Engineer. She was only seventeen, what if she became pregnant, would he have enough money to support her and a child?

Beatson and Flame were to be married in the same year and both were in favour of Lizzie giving her consent. Lizzie having been passionately in love with Locky herself, realised if permission was not granted, they could get carried away and an illegitimate child could arrive. Amela was not entirely aware of this. Nineteen fifty six was a wonderful year for any one who was in love. Beatson was in love, Flame was in love, Marie Louise was expecting her second child by the American Airman whom she had married the year before, and Alston had met his tall and lovely Scottish lass. It seemed every one she knew was in love. Even the famous beautiful American actress, Grace Kelly was marrying her Prince Rainier of Monaco

As far as the world was concerned, the government of Britain had launched their Premium Bond Scheme, buy a bond for a pound with a chance to win a million each month on the draw.

Earlier in the year the major cities of the country were shrouded in heavy blankets of fog, visibility being reduced to an arms length. It was not possible to drive a car, ride a bike or even walk the pavements without running the risk of hitting a person, or falling into canals or rivers. Thousands of people died as a result of bronchial illness and breathing difficulties. People were seen walking around with handkerchiefs up to their mouths and noses to filter the thick, black , polluted air they were forced to breathe.

The street lamps were barely visible through the dense fog that lay motionless across the major cities. Most homes had coal fires, belching out thick black smoke which hung around making the fog more dense and dangerous.

Returning from work in the dark was a hazardous operation. People removed their hanky masks and cosied up in their little homes. Due to the fact that for several previous years this night mare scenario took place, the Government brought in the Clean Air Act, forbidding scores of people and areas to burn coal, only smokeless fuel was permitted. As a result the following years were clean, no more killer smogs and fogs.

Britain was going to war with Egypt over the Suez canal, which President Nasser had closed. This would mean ships going round the Cape of Good Hope to bring the much sought after commodity of oil from the Middle East. Amela thought of her trip through the Canal barely two years before, she could not absorb the seriousness of the situation to Britain if the canal should remain closed, she barely knew that the Prime Minister of Britain was called Anthony Eden. All she could think of was her knight in shining armour who she was going to marry soon, her handsome and romantic Rex.

The marriage was a simple affair, Amela borrowed Marie Louise's wedding dress and veil. The Pastor of the tiny Pentecostal Church did not want the young couple to spend more than the barest minimum on a wedding ring. There were no bridesmaids, page boys, no large floral displays, no fancy wedding cake, no make up for the bride. The only person who owned a car amongst their acquaintances kindly offered to drive Beatson and Amela to the Church, every one else went by bus. The wedding was a tea total affair. Rex and Amela did not mind the lack of sophistication nor were they ashamed that their wedding was without pomp and ceremony. After a party like reception they were going back to Rex's home for the wedding night. They had booked a small two berth cabin cruiser on the Thames, for the honeymoon but were not to pick it up till the next day.

Rex had completed his five year apprenticeship the week before the ceremony. Between them they had very little money, but were sublimely happy knowing tonight was the night they would fulfil their deep desire.

A veil is drawn over the happenings of that night, sufficient to know, the young couple found out some weeks later that Amela was pregnant. Robert Barrington was a wedding night baby.

Amela and Rex went on to have another two children, a second boy was born to them five years later, and then 9 years later Amela gave birth to a baby girl. Their lives were very happy indeed. They were members of a local Church, and attended two or three times on a Sunday. The only thing that blighted their happiness was when Lizzie took ill and was found to be suffering from kidney cancer. The major operation was not successful, and after a course of radiation, she took to her bed and never recovered.

Amela, who had moved to Kent with Rex and her sons, would come up to London each weekend to see her mother. Lizzie spent her last few weeks in the house of Beatson and Inge. They were such sad days, no one wanted to speak, couldn't imagine life without their mother. The winter was one of the worst on record, the freeze had set in on boxing day of nineteen sixty three, and continued to the beginning of March. Amela went to visit her mother, knowing it would be the last time she would be making this journey.

She stood at the foot of her bed, "Bye Mum," she whispered, "I'll see you in the morning." Three days later the news of her mother's death arrived. The writer cannot describe the pain and grief she shared with her siblings that time.

Beatson, Alston and Gerry stood beside Flame and Amela by the side of Lizzie's grave. They had just sung the words of that beautiful hymn,

*"On that bright and cloudless morning when the dead in Christ shall rise,
And the glory of His resurrection share,
When the saved of old shall gather, over on the other side,
And the roll is called up yonder, I'll be there."*

Lizzie had been a tower of strength to all of them. She had taught them the true value of life, she had loved them all to the end. "When I am gone," she said, "Please stay together, love one another and bring your children up to be an active part in our privileged family."

Amela left the graveside and noticed the first crocuses in bloom. She placed her hand in Rex's outstretched hand and walked sadly and slowly to the waiting car.

The year was nineteen sixty three. Lizzie died at the age of sixty three. It was easy to remember this because she was born at the turn of the century.

Some time later on that year, on his daily commute from London, Rex returned to their home in Kent with a news paper advertising a job which he felt Amela would be good at. The Company called Nestles, was a leading manufacturer of chocolates, coffee and other top ranking food products in the U.K. and Europe. They were looking for interviewers for Kent and the South East of London. Amela had not returned to work since moving to their house in Kent some three years before, but felt this would be an ideal job. She would be able to pick and choose which surveys she wanted to take part in, and would be paid a handsome salary for doing this.

She asked the lady next door if she would be willing to take care of the children if and when she got the job. The interview was in London. On her return home after the interview, she was surprised to hear a neighbour say that she was unlikely to get the job because of her colour. Amela never gave her colour a thought. Why should anyone not give her a job that she would be most proficient at, because of her colour. If they turned her down it would be more likely that she could not drive a car, nor even owned one, certainly not because of her colour. Her ignorant neighbours struggled to speak English grammatically correctly, mixing up their "were" and "was" more frequently than one could imagine, "Colour indeed."

A few days later she received a letter advising her the job was hers. With her very first pay cheque, she enrolled for driving lessons. On her first lesson the driving instructor said he would repeat anything Amela found difficult to understand in the English language. "It is not the English language I find difficult to understand ," she said to him, "but the workings of the car." Was this going to be a pattern of things to come, was she constantly going to have to explain to people that her mother tongue was English despite the fact she was born in another country.

The job was an interesting one. She spent three or four days on each survey, going from house to house and interviewing people on soups, coffee, chocolates and instant tea. Her area stretched from Bromley and Lewisham in Kent to the coast near Dover, Sandwich and Ramsgate. Quite soon after her commencement with Nestles, she passed her driving test and acquired a car which simplified her duties, no more having to go by bus and train to the allotted area.

Round about this time, Enoch Powell had been reported to have made statements about the coloured people and the immigrants from the sub continent which caused unrest amongst the Brits. Immigrants were employed in the transport system and menial jobs in the health service. Britain desperately needed them. Ironic how a century before the British masses went to the sub continent to lay the great Indian railway network, and to the West Indies to manage the cotton plantations, and now when the roles were reversed the politicians were in an uproar.

Amela worked for Nestles for seven years, when she left because she was pregnant with her third child, the company wrote to her and said she was amongst their best interviewers, and if ever she wanted to return to work after the birth of the baby, the job would be hers.

During the time of her employment, one incident stands out because of the reaction of the woman on whose door she knocked. "Do you mind please Ma'am, sparing me a few minutes of your time and answering some questions on the subject of coffee.?"

"No, I will not," she said. Amela apologised for bothering her and turned to walk down the path. On reaching the gate, she heard the woman calling her, "Come back," she said. The woman was in the age range that Amela's survey required, so she was very glad to swallow her pride and return to the short tempered woman.

After the interview was over she poured her heart out to Amela."I used to foster a small child from Nigeria", she said, "I loved her and treated her as if she were my very own. When the little girl was ten years of age her parents wanted her back, I had to let her go, and with her went my heart."

The woman started to cry, "We did all we could for her and did not have one bit of hold on her against the parents who let her go when she was a baby. When I saw the colour of your brown face, I was reminded of that child, I'm sorry I was so abrupt and rude to you."

Amela worked on the subject of freeze dried coffee. One of the jobs she did, which she often refers to as her "baby" was the famous "Gold Blend." Another of the surveys she worked on, although with no success at all, was the subject of instant tea.

The British public had a thing about tea. It was conventionally made in a pot, allowed to stand and then poured after the milk had been poured, into china cups. Tea was within the reach of the common people, no more a commodity for the rich, the plantations that exported tea ranged from Darjeeling and Assam in the north of India to the Nilgiris in the South.

An Earl from Britain had added a spice to the conventional tea leaf and thus produced a special flavour which was more popular amongst the upper class of people. The question of class was slowly disappearing, and unlike generations before more and more common people were drinking the flavoured tea.

Anglo Indians were spreading across the world. Depending upon their education, their occupations and professions varied greatly. Indians continued their love of education and qualified in their hundreds as Medical Doctors, Consultants and General Practitioners.

The ancient caste system had been outlawed. Forgotten? Perhaps not.. Colour prejudice? No more? Who can tell. Religious resentment changed to tolerance ? One can but hope.

After seven years of working with Nestles, Amela fell pregnant with their third child. She never could understand how she conceived her first child on her wedding night, and went years before the next one and even longer before she fell for the third one.. She was delighted when her baby girl was born.

Each of the babies were born at home. Amela was afraid that if she had the babies in hospital, they might be accidentally changed and she could have been given someone elses baby . When the first child was born, the health authorities insisted the baby should be born in the hospital. Rex insisted that he should be in the room when Amela was giving birth. This was not to be allowed. The year was nineteen fifty seven and it was unheard of for fathers to be in the delivery room.

"Don't worry," he said to Amela. "If they don't give me permission to be with you, and if they insist you have to be in the hospital, we will not tell them when the time comes and I will deliver the baby myself."

This tuned out to be unnecessary. They did give Rex permission to stay with Amela, and they were happy to deliver the baby at home. At the time, when Amela had her first child, she was only eighteen years of age, Rex , just twenty two.

When their baby girl was born, their second son used to help the midwife with the bathing of the new born baby. He would hand her the cotton wool, the powder for the babies cord, and the clothes and blanket to wrap the little one in. The midwife asked what he would like to be when he grew up, he said "I'm going to be a doctor." Amela smiles when she remembers lying in bed and watching his gorgeous little face as he concentrated on his tiny baby sister. He was eight and a half year old.

Amela started a playschool to make sure her little girl did not grow up as an only child. The brothers were in school and to give the little one company she registered to run a group for eighteen children each morning. She called the school "Bedlam". Bedlam is another word for

Bethlehem, but in present day English it was synonymous with noisy happiness.

Rex built a large extension to their dining room to house the play school. To make full use of this room, Amela began running a Gospel Club in the evenings for young children up to the age of young teens. She taught the kids to sing choruses which she accompanied on her guitar, and told them stories from the Bible.

After a while, her sons began to bring home their friends, so Amela opened a youth club. The teenagers poured in. Some of them had not been to Church in their lives and knew nothing of the teachings of the Bible. Amela felt it a privilege to be doing this work for God. Her joy was complete when in later years, she knew one of the young men became a Vicar, another a Pastor of a non conformist Church and several others as youth leaders in their different communities. So many of them had given their hearts to the Lord as a result of the teaching they had received in the Gospel and Youth Clubs.

One day Rex and Amela were repairing a ceiling in the dining room when there was a knock on the door. Both of them were standing on chairs with their arms lifted to support the plaster board they were nailing to do the repair. One of the kids went to the door. A middle aged couple followed their son into the room. She had not seen them before, and had no idea who they were.

"I wont be a minute," Amela said, "Do sit down."

The man did not wait for Amela and Rex to finish what they were doing. "We are the parents of one of the lads that attend your Gospel Club," he said, "I have been watching the good work you have been doing with the children for a few years now and I am here to ask you to consider being nominated as a Justice of the Peace."

"What's a Justice of the Peace?" Amela asked.

"A Justice of the Peace, or another name for it is a Magistrate, is someone who is required to sit on the bench in the Courts and judge the people who come before them. There are several types of Magistrate courts, there is a Juvenile court, a Domestic Court and the Criminal courts."

Amela got down from the chair. "Only a magistrate can nominate another citizen to be considered for the magistracy, a citizen whose behaviour is exemplary,." said the man.

"It's a great honour, Amela", said Rex.

The man continued, "Ninety seven percent of all hearings are judged by the Magistrate courts, only three percent go on to the Crown Courts and are judged by a jury of twelve people before the Judge passes sentence."

Amela said nothing. The implication of the request did not sink in. "If you agree," continued the man, "I will submit your name to the Lord Chancellor's Office and some one will come and interview you at home. If you are accepted, you will be notified by letter from the Office in London and there will be a very formal swearing in ceremony at the Crown Court in Maidstone. However, if you are not accepted you will never know the reason why."

"I cant say "Yes" to your request, although I regard it as the honour Rex says it is, you see, I don't swear on the Bible or take an oath, and because of this, one has to accept my "Yes" as "Yes." I don't think the Chancellor of the Exchequer or any one else will accept this at the swearing in ceremony."

"You're wrong there, Ma'am, there is provision for people who are not prepared to take an oath of allegiance or do not want to swear on the Bible , it is called an "Affirmation."

The couple left. Amela accepted their request. After talking to Rex, she reeled under this great honour. Some weeks later two men called at the door. Amela was not expecting anyone and was dressed in a casual long flowery skirt and top. Her eldest son made a tray of tea for the guests while Amela continued with the interview.

Among a number of questions about her background, her occupation, her play school and her Gospel Clubs, they asked if she was prejudiced against the Police or long haired youths. "No," she said, "My dad was in the Police, and my son is a long haired youth." Amela did not know how the interview went. The two men were as serious as judges, and gave nothing away, anyway it was not up to them to accept or reject the candidate. Some months later, when she had forgotten all about it, Amela received a letter from the House of Lords, it read:

Madam,

Commission of the Peace for the County of Kent.

I am directed by the Lord Chancellor to inform you that you have been appointed a Justice of the Peace and that your name was placed on the above Commission on - -- and the date followed. It continues with an explanation of the logistics of taking the oath. It concludes,

I am, Madam,
Your obedient servant,
Secretary of Commissions.

The years that followed were increasingly interesting. Coincidently, the initials that now followed her surname , were the same as those that proceeded it. J.P----------J.P. She learnt a lot about life, the sadness, situations that were almost beyond her understanding, cases that in her sheltered life did not exist.

Protocol prevents her from relating cases or naming places and people. She learnt much from these sessions. She recalls a man who appeared before her charged for stealing under wear from washing lines, some one hundred and ten incidents were taken into consideration. In the court that day, was a class of sixteen year old students, who were visiting court as part of their education. They sniggered and giggled through out the hearing. The man's children were students in the same school. Can anyone imagine the humiliation this case brought to him and his family?

Another case that was brought to the Juvenile closed court was when two young boys were found taking coins from the town centre fountain. The court was unusually full for a closed court. Parents were allowed into such a court but the general public was not allowed in. As the hearing proceeded, the fathers of the boys , who were flanked by prison officers gave their testimony.

The Chairman of the bench leaned over and whispered in Amela's ear, "I sent him down for stealing lead off the Church roofs."

"Me, Lud," said one of the fathers, "I'd 'ave given 'im a clip round lug 'ole if I were at 'ome."

Amela tried hard to remain as serious as a judge.

At the year of her appointment there were only twenty one thousand Magistrates in the whole of the British Isles. The other thing that rather surprised Amela was how certain members of the family, who had previously thought of her as a scatter brained young thing, who hadn't finished her education and never earned a decent salary, who was married at the age of seventeen and spent her life surrounded by children, should be nominated and appointed as a Justice of the Peace. Suddenly she was being talked to as someone who might, after all, have a brain.

Locky would have been so proud of Amela, his fourth daughter, one he favoured because of her courage, who he probably recognised as having a special character. She was thirty six years old, beautiful, fashionable, probably one of the youngest J.P's in the country and almost certainly the only Anglo Indian.

Having served on the Bench for a few years, the couple moved to the north of England following a wish to be self sufficient. Fortunately the company Rex worked for, were setting up an office in Manchester and paid all expenses for the family to move. The agency fees, solicitors fees and removal fees were all taken care of, but it did mean giving up her seat on the bench and restarting as a magistrate in the north, an area she knew nothing about. It also meant saying good bye to her Gospel Club, her nursery school and the Youth club.

She declined the offer of starting as a magistrate in the North of England, she was going to be too busy with animals on the farm they purchased, and basically settling into an area which was entirely new to her. The farm was set twelve hundred feet up in the Pennines. She was constantly being asked why she left the balmy climate of Kent to come this remote , cold and bleak place. Her favoured reply, which she must have used a thousand times, was, "I left the garden of England to come to its backbone, and the warmth of the people here, more than makes up for the cold of the climate."

They settled into the farming life amid a host of hilarious incidents. Chasing sheep all over the moor, trying to shear them with a book on how to do it still in her hand, delivering lambs that were breach positioned, rearing calves on a single old Guernsey cow, visiting the local cattle markets and generally having a whale of a time.

But now it was nineteen eighty. Amela's sister Ruth May, was coming to England from Australia, she wanted to see all her British siblings, and how better than to see them all together. The last time Amela had seen Ruth May was twenty six years before, standing on the quay side as she waved goodbye to Lizzie, Amela and Gerry.

Gerry. The Musician.

The youngest child born to Lizzie and Locky was a boy named Gerry. He was the joy of Lizzie's life , born to her at the age of forty two. Just when she thought she had given up child bearing, believing herself to be going through the change of life, little Gerry was born. It was Gerry, four years younger than Amela who sat at her bedside when she had that near fatal accident, on the farm in Damoh. It was Gerry who travelled to England with Amela in the year nineteen fifty four. Gerry was just twelve at the time. It was Gerry who got so exasperated with every one in school telling him how good his English was, that he made up an answer telling people he had learnt to speak English on the boat coming over from India. He was full of good humour and a pleasure to be with. If one word could be found to sum up his personality, it would be ENTHUSIASM.

This poem is dedicated to Gerry.

The Death of a Cyclist.

The year is nineteen fifty five, the spring is setting in,
The winter is o'er, but what counts more,
Is that summer is over the brim.
He's just about twelve, this lad I know,
And his mind with promise is held
But his brain cannot think of paper and ink,
When his eyes a bike beheld.

As I told you before, 'twas fifty five,
The time went slipping by,
He was given a bike, which was pride to himself
And pride to the passer-by,
His life was enveloped by that frame on two wheels,
The brakes and the hub and the chain,
You could try to talk learning, or music or such,
But my friend you were talking in vain.

The year is nineteen fifty six,
The bike is a light weight one,
I'm quoting his words when I tell you this,
"But cycling is such good fun,"
But alas, I was busy with boyfriends and such,
And my hours you could hardly call mine,
But I studied this lad, and I watched him each day,
And I witnessed "A cyclist," in time.

The days and the weeks and the months just slipped by,
He was king of his domain.
His pump was his sceptre, his saddle his thrown,
And his subjects, his spokes and his chain.

To cycle to Cornwall or around the block,
His bike was his only means,
The craze just held fast and carried him through,
Till the year he was grown up fifteen.

But alas, my good friends there came a sad day,
When his eyes fell on Beatson's guitar.
He got off his bike, and held out his hands,
You could sense that the end wasn't far.
When he plucked at the cords and lifted his voice,
I realized that he also sings,
He'd caught the disease, the fatal disease,
That changed brakes for six miserable strings.

If you knew this lad, as I knew him then,
You'd know one thing for sure,
If he went in for something he'd got in his head,
He'd throw in his heart if not more,
So it wasn't surprising that as time went by
He acquired an instrument too,
When I looked at that frame, those wheels and the hub,
I felt unaccountably blue.

Time carried on, till in fifty seven,
The bike was just left in the hall,
Oh, he'd ride it my friends, please don't mistake that.
But that instrument seemed to rule all.
His life was released by that frame on two wheels,
The brakes and the hub and the chain,
But now if you spoke of music and such,
You wouldn't be talking in vain.

The disease took him fast and it held at his heart,
Until love for his bike was dead.

Instead of the oil and the grease and the pump,
He took his guitar to bed,
He played us some tunes and I'm happy to say,
It made him a different lad,
"The death of a cyclist", in him did I find,
But somehow it didn't seem bad.

"The death of a cyclist", but the birth of a king,
A king in a different domain,
Instead of a pedal, a guitar he held,
And harked to the pretty notes strain.
A king is his right, in a different way,
Where he lives for his music and song,
I'm certain that cyclist as he lies in his grave ,
Whispers, "King, I hope you live long."

Gerry went from strength to strength with his guitar playing. After he finished his education in a school in South London, Lizzie insisted he took up an apprenticeship. He began work at the Kingston Power Station and spent the next five years qualifying as an instrument engineer. During this time he met a lovely young lass and fell hopelessly in love with her. "Her legs go all the way up to paradise", he told Amela one day. Amela could guess what he meant by "paradise." The day he finished his apprenticeship, he jacked in his job and became a professional musician.

At first his gigs were in local clubs, barmitsvahs, weddings and parties. He progressed then to performances in clubs in London, and the home counties. He bought himself a Martin guitar, at that time there were only four of these guitars in England, Gerry and Beatson owned one each. They cost hundreds of pounds, probably the deposit for a three bed roomed house in South London. Gerry was totally confidant that he could earn a handsome living with his blues singing and the guitar playing. He married the Paradise girl, who went on to give him two lovely sons.

Gerry wrote many of his own songs. He used to do the summer seasons on the island of Jersey where he became well known. He performed in most of the major countries in Europe, earning a substantial amount of money. He played in Madison Square gardens in New York and many cities in the United States. His long playing vinyl. records were selling very well, and Gerry was making quite a name for himself. At that time, a music magazine printed a survey of the worlds top artists, they asked the question as to who these world renowned performers thought was, in their opinion, the best musician in the world. The famous guitarist and singer, Eric Clapton, named Gerry Loughran as his number one musician.

Because of the difficulty in pronouncing the name of Loughran when seen written on a poster or hoarding, Gerry changed his surname to his stage name of Lockran. Amela remembers the Christmas Gerry spent with her, it was strange seeing him on the television when he was sitting beside her on the settee.

The family did not realize just how successful he was. One summer Rex and Amela took their little boys camping. They drove to Bulgaria, Yugoslavia, and then through Greece ,on to Turkey. On the way back, Amela noticed a hitch hiker sitting in a lay by in Turkey, he was playing a guitar. She moved the boys to one side, and packed the young singer in with his back pack and his guitar. As they journeyed, they began talking about travels and music, to which Amela asked who his favourite singer was. "Oh, you wont know him," he said, he is well known in the blues world but not well known in pop music, he's called Gerry Lockran." Amela gulped in amazement, "Would it surprise you to know that Gerry Lockran is my brother?"

Much of Gerry's chapter is mixed with Amela. The two of them were the nearest in age and shared many of their childhood and youth experiences. Amela loved Gerry, he thought she was fabulous.

But now it is nineteen eighty. "Stop every thing you are doing Gerry, don't arrange any more gigs for the dates I am telling you, Ruth May is coming from Australia and we haven't seen her for twenty six years. I want the whole family to be here to greet her, bring the boys and the Paradise girl and what ever you do, don't forget your guitar."

Chapter 11
Memories of the Raj

The year is nineteen eighty. A newspaper write up and an enlarged photograph hangs on the dining room wall. It is of some thirty five people, ranging in age from seven year old kids to some approaching their fifties, all looking extremely happy, the title reads, MEMORIES OF THE RAJ. High up in the backbone of England, no more than a mile or so from the famous Pennine Way, a local newspaper reporter visited a farm house to record the reunion of the Loughran family.

Looking down across the valley, one could see the ranges of hills that constitutes the Pennines, the range of hills that make up the backbone of England. The higher you are, the better the view, they say, and so it was from Higher Mount, sitting twelve hundred feet up on a south facing hillside. The view across the valley was unbroken, miles and miles of country side could clearly be seen. Sheep in their thousands grazed the marginal land on both sides of the valley. A characteristic feature of this breath taking scenery was the miles of dry stone walls that enclosed the fields, built many hundreds of years ago by farm labourers. Most of the dry stone walling still stood in tact, but where it had fallen down it was often replaced by sheep netting, a commodity that was cheaper and easier to erect, but not so scenic nor so effective in keeping the flocks within their own pastures.

Here and there one could observe a herd of cows munching peacefully on the fresh green grass on the hills, or a horse which farmers and small holders kept as pets for their children. High in the sky, swooping and darting in all directions was a number of house martins, their nests hung perilously from the eaves of the house. It was a beautiful summer's day, the atmospheric pressure was high, causing midges to fly high above the fields. The house martins whose main diet was midges also flew high in the sky, they would swoop at an amazing speed and dart into their nests to supply their open mouthed young with continual feed.

The photographer tried hard to get the guests to bunch together for the photograph, but no one was heeding his instructions. The family were so excited to see one another, "Will every one please stand in front of the house," he pleaded, "little ones kneel in front of your mums and dads, the tallest ones go to the back." Amela. In her authoritative manner managed to get them to listen to the photographer and pose for this memorable photo.

A multitude of cars filled the car park, trailers and tents were dotted around the fields nearest the house, even the sheep, the geese and the cattle came near to investigate the change around the farm house.

Steele, who was absent from the re-union, sent his son and daughter, to represent him, as an airline pilot he had seen Ruth May many times and it was not imperative that he should be there.

Ruth May was over whelmed by the reception she received from the siblings and their children. She was melancholy when she thought of the years they had spent apart and the path her life had taken. Her marriage had not turned out well, she had dedicated her life to looking after and raising her six children, who were her joy and reward in life. Her eyes filled with tears when she told Gerry and Amela how she felt when she waved them goodbye at the quay side in Bombay. "I knew I would never see our mother again," she said, wiping away her tears, "I didn't think I would ever see you two again either. But here I am, with all of you, and how happy and grateful I feel." Amela too started to cry, tears of memory and joy, tears of regret and failure, tears of success and achievement.

Beatson drove his family down from Scotland. He had been transferred from London to the Giro Bank situated in Glasgow. When Lizzie had died she asked him to keep the whole family together, and so he did. He was blissfully happy with his German wife Inge and their four children, it was truly a marriage made in heaven. Because of his love for, and his natural ability in music, his children became proficient musicians. They brought guitars, mandolins and violins with them.

Marie Louise seemed to be lost forever to the rest of the family. Try as they might, they were unable to trace her in her new home in America, so sadly she and her family were missing from the Memories of the Raj.

Alston and Rea came up from Bristol, along with their three lovely children. Alston, who was a real family man, was overjoyed to see his oldest sister Ruth May. Their eldest son showed off the fabulous caravannette he had made, he later married the pretty young girlfriend he brought with him. Years later this young man was called into the bank manager's office and he was told he was a registered as an official millionaire.

Flame drove up from London with her two sons and her new husband Jim. To all around she was getting over her marriage break up with Peter, but deep down in her heart she remembered the happy years they spent together with their two little sons. She brought huge containers full of different types of curry and pilau, and prepared to make parathas and other Indian delicacies once she had greeted the rest of the family.

Amela, who was the organiser, had posted time tables and schedules for serving and clearing away on various places on the Dining Room Wall. It became a competition as to which group could serve the meals best. In their normal dramatic way, the Loughrans and their families all rose to the occasion.

Gerry brought his Paradise girl and their two sons. Amela needn't have reminded him to bring his guitar, he never went any where without it, it was like another limb to his body.

During each day the family went out to various places of sport, horse riding and rambling across the Yorkshire moors. Each day was more special than the last, and every member of the family remembered these times for the rest of their lives.

In the evening, after a sumptuous meal, they would gather in the lounge, which over flowed to capacity, and sang and played instruments till the early hours of the morning. These were parties the likes of which they had not seen before nor would see again on this scale. Ruth May the Soprano entertained her younger siblings with songs she learnt at Locky's knee. Her voice still retaining its power and volume.

> *"I saw a peaceful old valley,*
> *With a carpet of corn for the floor,*
> *And I heard a voice within me whisper,*
> *This is worth fighting for.*
> *Didn't I build that cabin,*
> *Didn't I plant that corn,*
> *Didn't my loved ones before me,*
> *Fight for the country in which I was born,*
> *I gathered my loved ones around me,*
> *I gazed at each face I adored,*
> *And I heard a voice within me thunder,*
> *This is worth fighting for."*

The words rang out loud and clear, it was almost as if Locky himself were singing to them. She recalled her solo at the celebration on Independence day, when she was eighteen years of age, and had not felt the hardship of her later years. O yes, there were memories and there were tears. Precious memories and precious tears.

Then it was Gerry's turn. They say a prophet is not without honour save in his own country and in his own home. None of the group realized how good a musician Gerry was, nor how he was making a name for himself in professional circles. Gerry wrote many of the songs himself, his guitar playing was second to none in the world. Sufficient to say that his audience thoroughly enjoyed his entertainment. Word got round the neighbourhood that he was in town, and for the rest of the week a number of friends and neighbours dropped in to the party.

Without exception, every one thought of this as an unusual gathering, the newspaper reported it as such. A family from the highest mountain range in the world now gathering together in the Pennines to celebrate and remember the great British Raj.

Amela took Rex's hand, he was not in it, love him as she did, he was not in it. Memories of one's parents, family, youth and the country of one's birth, MEMORIES OF THE RAJ , no, he was not in it. This special time belonged to Ruth May, Beatson, Alston, Flame , Amela and Gerry.

There was a certain sadness when the family disbanded and returned to their homes , continuing with the occupations that made their lives so warm and comfortable in the world. Rex and Amela continued with the self sufficiency they so desired. Friends and family from all over the country continued to spend their summer holidays with them on the farm, helping as best they could to make things easier.

The book they lived by was written by one John Seymour, it taught them pretty well all they knew on self sufficiency. He taught them how to milk a goat, to sheer a sheep, to deliver a baby animal if the mother was having difficulty in giving birth due to the fact the young one was lying in a breach position. He taught them how to bottle feed and hand rear a lamb if the mother had three lambs born to her. He taught them how to grow potatoes without having to pile the soil around the young plants, he taught them how to force rhubarb so as it was edible when the weather was still cold. He taught them about crop rotation, about tilling and irrigating the ground for best results. He taught them how to do all these things without the need of electricity, or any mechanical instruments.

As far as the kitchen was concerned, he taught them how to take the clotted cream off the rich milk produced from a Guernsey cow, how to allow the mother cow to adopt a second calf so as to use up the surplus milk that her own calf could not manage to consume. He taught them all about geese, hens and guinea fowl.

Rex and Amela had a goat they bought when they were still in Kent, unbeknown to them , the goat which they called Deborah was with kid when they bought her. By the time they brought her up to West Yorkshire, the kids were no longer suckling from her, but she was still producing milk. Rex and Amela decided to milk the goat and make a soft cheese which they read was very good for the health. They tried tying her up in the cow shed, Rex held her horns while proffering her a bucket full of fodder. Deborah ate the fodder and stood quite still while Amela held a bucket between her knees and proceeded to milk the goat. Just as she was finishing the task, Deborah broke away from Rex's grasp, kicked the bucket away from Amela's knees, and sent the milk flying.

The next day, Beatson and the family were arriving from Scotland for their summer holiday. "We'll let her into the field ", said Rex, "We'll milk her outside, we don't want the Scots to think we don't know anything about farming." The Scottish cousins joined Amela's own children to help with the milking of Deborah. Each young person took hold of a leg, Rex held her horns and Amela set to, to do the milking. As Deborah had finished eating the fodder, she shook Rex off her horns, kicked her legs so the young people let her go, and then gave one big hoof which kicked the milk bucket out from between Amela's knees and sent her sprawling onto the grass.

"Oh, I don't think we'll bother with her any more ," said Rex, she will dry up on her own when she is ready." Amela got up, shook herself free of the mud and grass and went with her empty pail into the house.

"The sheep need sheering, lets get the youngsters to help us, "said Rex. "We'll start with Rastus, the ram." Rastus and five ewes were purchased from a flock of Jacob sheep, renowned for their black and white wool which was ideal for home spinning. Rastus had been hand reared as a lamb, and regarded humans as one of his own species. He was a splendid creature with two large straight horns and two curling horns. Rex and Amela took the necessary equipment out into the field to sheer Rastus. The equipment constituted a mat, a pair of scissor sheers and the book by John Seymour open at the appropriate page.

Rex sat Rastus on the mat between his legs, holding him with one hand so that he could easily access his under side. Amela held the book while the kids looked on in admiration.

"Make the first cut under his throat, open the wool downwards." Amela read the instructions to Rex. "Remember the wool has to come off in one piece. About one hour later, with the wool in a hundred pieces the job was done. Rastus looked awful, more like a ploughed field than a sheered sheep. They began to chase the flock in a vain attempt to catch the next victim for sheering. They tried every thing, the young folk were running in every direction with no success, the sheep were just out of grasp, jumping over the stone walls and bleating pitifully. Amela's nephew said , "Uncle Rex, I do think we are doing something wrong, there must be an easier way," he turned and walked disgustedly back to the farm house.

Rex filled his bucket and tempted the six remaining sheep into the cow shed where he made a small enclosure catching each sheep more easily than the chase around the field. It took an average forty five minutes to sheer each sheep. At the same time there was a programme on television showing how the Australian sheep sheerers took forty five seconds to do the same job. The following year they hired the boys on the next farm to do the job for them.

During the lambing season, they noticed one of the sheep was having difficulty giving birth. They put her in the cow shed into a special pen which Rex had made for such an eventuality. It was dark with no electricity in the cow shed. This time there were no helpers, only their young daughter Ruth, "Come on darling , we'll have to go and help Lucky the sheep give birth to her babies." Ruth held the lantern, while Rex stood at the sheep's head speaking in a tender voice to the old girl. "Alright Lucky, it wont be long now." Amela had removed her rings from her right hand and with book in hand went out to the cowshed. In the dim light of the lantern she knelt behind Lucky, then gritting her teeth and crying in fear, she began to put her hand into the sheep. Its one thing to read about what to do in a book, but quite a different thing to be actually doing it. It was warm and wet inside Lucky, she could see and feel the head of the lamb but not its feet. Seymour had said, you must push the head back, hook your fingers round the turned back feet and pull them out so that the head is now resting on the hoofs. When the natural and correct position is gained, allow the sheep to give birth to her lamb.

Within minutes of adjusting the position of the lamb, it plopped out onto the hay. Lucky licked it, baaing softly. The three of them went back into the house to recover from this exciting ordeal. A half hour later Amela went out to see what was happening. Imagine her delight when she saw a second lamb on the hay, Lucky was licking this lamb to remove the natal membrane. Amela could see the birth canal was still open, she shone the torch onto Lucky and was not only surprised but delighted to see the emergence of a third lamb.

Amela felt as if she truly was a shepherdess Extra Ordinaire.

They never did manage to grow potatoes without having to earth them up, or to force rhubarb so that it could be picked in the early spring. John Seymour had no idea how cold it was for the most part of the year way up high in the Pennines.

Rex and Amela had a wonderful time and learnt much from their farm experience. Rex continued to work in Manchester and it fell to Amela to run the farm as best she could during the week. They continued to do this for several years until Amela decided to go back to work also, so they sold their live stock and rented the field to a neighbouring farmer.

Amela went for interview to a company in the northern town of Todmorden. She wore an elegant navy blue pin striped dress with three long strands of pearls which she bunched together in a knot. Her long dark hair was neatly styled in a French pleat and secured behind her head. Her make up was barely visible and her nails manicured and varnished with a pale pink lacquer. This was in direct contrast to the way she looked when she was delivering lambs or sheering sheep.

The company manufactured riveting tools and traded in electronic components. Their products were sold to hundreds of companies in the U.K., and exported to many countries in the world. They were looking for a person with an air of confidence about them who would be responsible as a public relations assistant to the Managing Director. The interview lasted but a few minutes. Amela answered the questions put to her and quickly covered the experience she had gained in her previous jobs. The young man who conducted the interview shook hands with Amela and said he would be in touch with her and let her know if the job was hers.

He then hurried in to the office of the Managing Director, "I've found her, I've found her, " he said. "She is just what you are looking for."

"Is she good looking and elegant , smartly dressed and wearing yards of pearls.?" the boss enquired. "Does she speak perfect English? does she have confidence about her that would be obvious when she meets business clients for the first time, is she middle aged and not a giggly young thing.?" "She is every thing you want Mr.T."

"Then write to her and offer her the job." he said.

Amela started work within a few a days She met the Boss for the first time, he was not what she expected judging from the tall young man that conducted the interview. Mr. T was about seventy years old, a short man with balding hair, he had the head of Adonis. The look about his eyes conveyed some sad incidents in his life. He was dressed in plain ordinary clothes, and gave the impression of being very down to earth. As time went on, he told Amela that he was a Jew , and had lived in Germany during the years that preceeded the war. He had fled Germany to live in Manchester when he was only fifteen years old.

He bought himself a suitcase and filled it with tools, hammers, spanners, screw drivers and the likes and literally went from door to door trying to sell them. As time went on, the superiority of his brain came to the fore, and he began to invent hand held riveting tools. He called this commodity King Klik, it began to sell extremely well, so he purchased a factory in the town of Todmorden, and began selling King Klik nationwide. It soon became a house hold word. Later on, as technology progressed, and electronic components were required to run plant and machinery of all kinds, he began trading in these also. Not only did he send them to points in the U.K., but he also had a world wide market. With hard work, and a dedication that defies description, Mr. T. became a multi millionaire.

Often Amela would sit and talk to him about his life, and about her own. He told her his parents had been in a concentration camp in Germany. He had been sent to a relative who lived in Manchester and had escaped the torture of the holocaust. He never heard from his parents again, he only knew they were sent to the gas chamber and died with the other millions of Jews in that country.

"Has this affected your life Mr.T" Amela asked him one day. "I think about it a lot, perhaps not every day, but the loss of my parents and the way in which they died is never far from my mind," he replied.

"Do you know anything about the Jewish faith?, he asked Amela. "Yes of course, I do, Mr. T., my Saviour was a Jew, He was the greatest person this world has ever known."

"So that makes you a Christian, Amela?." "Yes, it does, most definitely," she answered.

"I am not a practising Jew, I haven't been to a synagogue for many, many years, "he said, "Would you like to come with me, if I decided to go," he said. Amela, who was deeply interested in the Jewish faith, accepted this invitation without hesitation. It never did come to anything. Mr.T did not go to a synagogue again and so Amela was left in anticipation. She often reflected on this situation, her grandmother Pushpa had been a Hindu, her mother Lizzie and herself devout Christians, and here she was enjoying being employed by a Jew, and conversing with him at great length about faith, about faith of any description.

One day, Mr .T. quoted a verse from the Bible, the old Testament. "That verse comes from the Book of Psalms, do you know anything about the Old Testament Amela?" Amela nearly started laughing, "Mr. T. I have been studying the Scriptures, Old and New Testaments diligently for many years now, I have to tell you that verse does not come from the Book of Psalms, but from the Book of Job."

"No, it doesn't , I was taught in school that it came from the Book of Psalms, " he continued.

"I don't care where you were taught Mr. T. you were taught wrong, that verse you just quoted me comes from the Book of Job."

"Bet you," he said, "Bet you a fiver."

"Okay," said Amela, I am not a betting person, but since this is a certainty, I'll take you on, a fiver then." Amela went home during the lunch hour and collected her Bible, she found the appropriate verse and left the Book open on Mr.T's desk.

When he returned after lunch, and saw the open Bible, he looked doe eyed into Amela's face, put his hand in his pocket and handed her the five pound note. Word soon got round the factory and offices that Mr. T had lost money to one of his employees.

Amela was extremely fond of Mr. T. He seemed to terrify the others with his severe and austere look. Stalking the works, making people jump to attention, pretending as if they were working even if they were taking a five minute breather. Often on a Friday afternoon, when orders ceased to come in by phone, fax or in person, Amela would take a quiz book into work and ask her colleagues trivial pursuit questions. One day, Mr T. walked in whilst Amela was in the middle of a question, the others put their heads down in an effort to show him they were still at work, Amela turned to Mr. T. and said "Right Mr. T. this question is for you," he was so flabbergasted he answered without hesitation and because he enjoyed this little game continued to stay in the office to answer more questions.

Amela made several friends whilst working at Mr.T. place, people who remained close friends with her for the rest of her life. She would meet with them every few weeks where they would either order in a curry from the local take away or gorge themselves on the delightful cuisine made by Joyce, Margaret or Mary Anne.

One day, on returning to the farm after work, the phone was ringing. Amela was silenced to hear Flame's husband Jim at the other end of the line. Flame's eldest son had gone to India on his honeymoon, they had just received a phone call from his new bride to say that Steven had contracted meningitis, the situation was serious, and she feared the worst. "Please don't ring ", he said, "We have been asked to keep the line clear so we could be informed of any change in his condition." Amela replaced the phone. Her heart sank, she knew little about meningitis, she telephoned her young son who had recently qualified as a Doctor and told him the news. "What can we expect son?" she asked . "It's very hard to say Mum," just keep the line clear so Jim could ring you with the news, hopefully of Steven having passed the crisis."

Amela could think of nothing else and prayed that Steven would recover. The next evening, when the phone rang and she heard Jim's voice, she said nothing, just replaced the receiver after hearing him tell her that Steven had died. It was the saddest day in Amela's life. One is not programmed to lose one's child. A parent of course, a sibling perhaps, maybe even your husband, but not one's child.

She wrote a letter to Flame, one to Steven's younger brother, one to Jim, and one to the young widow, but Amela was totally unable to pick up the phone and speak to her sister. She loved Flame so much and felt her grief. She could not find words to talk to her, all she could do was write her a letter. It was October nineteen eighty seven.

Steven died when he was twenty nine years old.

That summer had been uneventful. As usual friends and relations came to visit and spend their holidays on the farm. Gerry had been up too, but he was not his usual vivacious self. Gerry had had a heart attack when he was on stage some five or so years before, he too almost lost his life, but recovered sufficiently to live in the slow lane rather than the fast lane of life which he was used to.

During the days in hospital, Gerry had a stroke which left the left side of his body paralysed , he was unable to play his guitar ever again. He was in a wheel chair and fought to regain his mobility. His wife, who we always referred to as his Paradise girl, took the greatest care of him as did his two sons. He took up photography, and has been mentioned before the characteristic that best described Gerry, enthusiasm, surrounded this new found hobby. He took prize winning shots of the scenery surrounding the farm, sending enlargements to his sister Amela to hang on the dining room wall.

The autumn was over shadowed with the tragic news of Steven's death. Amela could not think of anything else, and as the weeks progressed she still could not find it in herself to speak to Flame.

On returning home from work one evening, her young daughter greeted her with the words, "Mum, I'm so sorry, I have bad news for you, I'm so sorry Mum." "What is it ," Amela asked. "I'm so sorry, Mum," she was crying, "I'm so sorry Mum." Amela began to panic, "What is it, " she said her voice rising , "Mum, I'm so sorry," Amela thought of Flame's terrible loss and thought of her own two sons. She was almost hysterical when she shouted at her daughter, "What is it, what is the news?"

"Your brother Gerry is dead."

Amela sat down on the stairs, "Is that all", She said. The relief flooded over her brain when she knew it was not either of her sons. She sat on the stairs with her head in her hands. How long she sat there no one knows, her daughter brought her a cup of tea, "Here you are Mum, drink this ," she said. "My brother Gerry is dead, my little brother Gerry is dead," she was heard to repeat these words over and over again and again. "My little brother Gerry is dead," she cried uncontrollably. The awful news began to sink into her, her precious little brother was dead, the one she had shared so much of her life with, the one who was with her when she stopped breathing in that hospital .operating room in India, the one whose enthusiasm and love of life had lasted long after the incident that put an end to his professional musical career. There was so much more to Gerry than his ability to play a guitar, his personality and warmth was rare and would be missed terribly, Amela would never get over the loss of her brother. He was only forty five years of age, what a tragic loss, what a waste.

The telephone kept ringing, call after call which Amela answered. It was Beatson, then Alston, Ruth May rang from Australia, then Steele from where ever he was at the time. Each one of them mentioned that they had received a letter during the past fort night from Gerry. Amela wondered why he hadn't written to her, he usually did, often sending her photographs which he had recently taken. Beatson was going to officiate at the funeral of his youngest brother, it was set for the following Monday.

Amela spent the next few days making a wreath in the shape of a guitar to lay on his coffin. She bought masses and masses of chrysanthemums , cut off the stalks and set them in a bed of oasis.

On the Saturday morning before the funeral, she received a letter which Gerry had written and posted two hours before he died. It was so typical of him, funny and entertaining. He addressed her as his "Dear and fabulous sister." it went on to read, "Don't you love and care for your little brother in Surrey, why haven't you written or phoned me for so long?" He mentioned that Flame was doing okay after the death of Steven which only happened six weeks before this, he also said he was three hundred percent in his soul and never ever intended to give up laughing.

Bobbi his wife took him to the post box to post the letter, he then went upstairs, said he was tired, and died in his bed. Parts of the letter were read by Beatson at his funeral. After the service, during which they sang the words of that wonderful and famous hymn,"

> "When the trumpet of the Lord shall sound,
> And time shall be no more,
> And the morning breaks eternal bright and fair,
> When the saved of old shall gather over on the other shore,
> And the roll is called up yonder I'll be there".

After the internment, they all returned to Gerry's home. Flame sat next to Amela in the car that took them to the crematorium. She took hold of her hand, "It's alright Amela," she whispered, "I'm doing okay, please don't think you have to stop ringing me, I want you to talk about Steven as if he were still alive."

Amela could not stop crying, her grief was for Flame and the death of Steven and the loss they both felt at Gerry's death. On arrival back at Gerry's house, his music from his umpteen records sounded throughout the rooms and garden, one could almost imagine he would walk through the door at any time. Hanging on the dining room wall was his Martin guitar, the one he had purchased at the commencement of his career. Bobbi had notified all his friends, Royd Rivers a musician he had performed with for a number of years, and others who were his big fans were all at his funeral. Amongst the guests was a professional photographer. He set the siblings in a group, there were five of them present for the picture. Ruth May was unable to come from Australia, and of course no one knew where Marie Louise was. The picture is a classic, printed in black and white, showing all five of them, beautifully dressed, elegant and good looking, all proud of the youngest one who was now no longer with them.

But life goes on. Their young daughter was thinking of leaving home, moving into the town, away from the farm, buying a little place for herself. It would be easier for her to journey from there to her place of work in the city of Bradford. Their eldest son who had never come up to live on the farm but remained in the south of England, had now moved to Canada, where he was taking a Master's degree and going on to do a Ph.D in psychology and Philosophy. Their second son who was now a fully qualified doctor, bought a house in the University city of Liverpool where he lived with his girl friend, a lovely red haired young girl whom he fell in love with when he was at school in the Calder Valley, West Yorkshire. She too went to university at the same time as he did and qualified as a doctor on the same day.

Rex and Amela decided to sell the farm and move to a place that would be easier to access during the snow filled winters. It was a sad day for both of them when they walked up the drive to the car and the removals van. "Don't look back darling," he said to her, holding her hand and quite literally dragging her up to the waiting car. "We'll be fine once we have settled into our new home, we've had such a wonderful time here, such happiness and sadness, so many new experiences and have learnt so much in life, come on, cheer up, our new life is only just beginning."

Chapter 12
Leprosy

Their new home was in the neighbouring county of Lancashire. Another county with stunning scenery. It was unlike the rugged bleak Yorkshire moors on which the farm was situated but every bit as beautiful in a different way. Their new home which had been a beer house in the last century had been converted into a family residence. Like most of the properties of that age, it still needed a lot of renovation and restoration. Rex and Amela who were quite used to that sort of thing, having done a lot of it in their previous homes, quite relished the idea.

Amela drove back each day to the town of Todmorden to continue her job as pubic relations with Mr. T. She tried hard to make her new house her home, but she sadly missed the company of her young daughter who by now was settled into a little terrace house in the town. She had not as yet visited the new residence, like her parents she was busy making a home for herself. A few days later she drove over to see how her Mum and Dad were getting on. She bounced in like a breath of spring air, rushing through the rooms to see where her mother had put what. She pivoted around and swung her arms in all directions, "I love it Mum," she said. She began rummaging in her mother's cupboards to find a jumper, a skirt or a pair of trousers. Amela began to smile, I feel at home now, she thought, just knowing this girl likes our place and feels at home here herself.

A few days later Amela went in to see Mr. T in his office. "Could I have a rise please Mr. T?" she asked. "No Amela," he replied. She turned on her heel and left the office. "Amela come back ," he called, "Let me tell you why you cant have a rise." "I don't want to know why I cant have a rise, its enough to know that you will not give me one." She was determined in her mind to look for another job. She drove the eighteen miles home that evening. Rex arrived a few minute later, "Lets go and get a take away," he suggested, "We'll drive round and learn a bit about the district.

Whilst waiting for the take away to be prepared, Rex picked up the news paper that lay on the counter. "Look at this advert Amela, " he said, "this job is written for you." She read what Rex was pointing out to her, she did not understand a bit about it, "Wanted, North West Regional Manager for a third world leading charity, the charity serves leprosy sufferers with a view to eradication of the disease before the turn of the century. The successful applicant will be familiar with fund raising, public speaking, running social events and generally raising the profile of the charity. Please telephone ……..for an application form."

"I cant do that Rex," Amela objected. "For one thing, I don't know any thing about charities, and the only public speaking I have done is at Churches, Gospel clubs and women's meetings on the subject of Christianity."

"Have you got a pen on you, " Rex asked. "I want to jot down this telephone number, besides all that, I think you are driving far too much to Todmorden each day, this regional office is in the town near to where our new home is." "This is all I have", she replied, handing him a lipstick. Using the lipstick as a pen, he scribbled the number on a brown paper bag that was lying on the counter, they picked up their curry and rice and drove home.

The next day Amela telephoned for the application form. If Rex thought she was suitable for the Managerial position, she'd give it a go. After all there was no prospect here for an increment, and the salary the

Charity was offering was better than what Mr. T, was giving her. She filled in the four page application form without reading the instructions. When she re-read it she found the words written at the head of the form, "Please use black pen." Amela had filled the whole form in with blue pen, she telephoned the head office and told them what she had done, "Don't worry", they said, "We request this because it is easier to read when it is photo copied."

Amela was called for interview. On her arrival at a hotel in Birmingham, she was told that eleven applicants had been short listed for two regional positions, there had been a total of one hundred and five applicants for the job. The day long interview was adjudicated by four senior employees of the charity. The two sessions before lunch, took the form of public speaking. Each applicant had to speak for five minutes on a charity, and four minutes about themselves. If perchance you overshot your time limit the adjudicators would raise their arms and you would be forced to discontinue your speech and take your seat again.

Amela was the oldest by many years. The smart young contestants ranged from pretty young business women to highly educated young men. One by one the names were called, Amela was interested in their speeches, they were certainly more knowledgeable in charities than she was, one of them spoke on the Royal Society for the Protection of Birds, one spoke about the Samaritans, another about Saving the whales., they had all worked for charities before and had experience of how things were done. Then Amela heard her name called.

"Ladies and Gentlemen", Amela began her speech." The other day I received a phone call from a young man in Canada, "I've had quite a day at work today", he said, "I was working in a psychiatric hospital when I met a young girl who was self harming, she had cut herself with a knife which left gashes up her forearm"

"What did you do?" Amela asked him, "I did what I could Mum, I took the sharp instrument away from her and talked to her.

"A day or two later" Amela continued, "a young man came in from his holiday job and threw his brief case into the cupboard under the stairs,

"I've had quite a day at work today", he said as he sat down with a cup of tea. I was asked to give an injection of sedation to a psychiatric patient.

"As I was preparing his arm for the injection, he kept mumbling the words, "You're good to me, you're good to me, you're good to me you're good to me," then completely by surprise he knocked the syringe clean out of my hand and sent it flying across the ward, he shouted "I'll break your bloody arm."

"What did you do?" she asked him "I did what I could Mum, I picked up the syringe, got a replacement sterile one and sedated him."

A week or so later, a beautiful young girl, who was awaiting her A level results took up a job in the local Psychiatric hospital as a cleaner. When she came home one evening, she said, "Oh, I've had quite a day at work today, I was cleaning the ward when Sophie came in, she started rubbing soap in her eyes and chewing the curtains." What did you do" Amela asked. "I did what I could Mum," she said, I took the soap away from her and led her to a room where there were no curtains."

Amela continued, "Little is known about mental illness. Please do what you can and contribute to the charity. I thank you for your attention and your response." She sat down.

There was silence in the room. The appeal had taken about four minutes, during which time the audience was riveted by Amela's speech. When the adjudicators had regained their composure, one of the applicants was heard to say, "How do we follow that one?" The interview continued.

The next phase was to talk for four minutes on one's own life. The speeches were rambling and boring, many of the applicants had over shot their allotted time and were requested to take a seat before they had finished. Amela heard her name being called. She rose to face the adjudicators and the other contestants.

"I was born in India", she began, "the seventh child and the youngest daughter to my parents. My paternal grand parents came from Ireland and Russia, my maternal grandparents from England and India. My illustrious English grand father was disinherited when he fell in love with and married my Hindu grandmother. I am known as an Anglo Indian.

I was educated in the foothills of the Himalayas in a prestigious English boarding school. When I finished my education I came to England, to a land where I could be understood, and where I am completely at home. My mother tongue is English. My commercial education was completed at Pitman's college in South Wimbledon. I am married to a wonderful English man and have been blessed with three wonderful children.

If you were to ask me what my life's work was, it would be very easy for me to tell you. My life's work are my three children., every thing and every one else in the world comes second to them,." she sat down.

After lunch, there was a letter writing test. The applicants had to write a letter of thanks to some one who had contributed to their charity. This did not pose a problem to Amela who had been writing letters from school to her parents on a weekly basis, the habit continuing long into her later life when she would pen letters to her family and friends.

The fourth and final part of the days interview took the form of a krypton factor type test. The applicants were divided into two teams, Amela was made captain of one. A pile of different coloured plastic shapes were placed in the centre of a table around which the members of each team sat Outside the conference room, set in the corridor, was a model made of similar coloured plastic shapes. The groups each had to copy the shape that was outside. There were only two rules to the game, 1) only one person at a time was allowed out side the conference room in the corridor, 2) the other rule was, no one had to ask the rules. The winner would be the first team to finish the project, there was no time limit.

Amela sent one of her team out to mentally copy the design of the model in the corridor, then come in and explain what colour lay where, and how many of the pieces were piled upon each other. When her team member re-entered the room, the other side sent out a member to do the same thing. This went on several times, then Amela had an idea, lets take the table outside to the corridor. We'll manipulate it so as only one of our group is outside in the corridor whilst the others of us can handle the table inside the room. "We cant do that," said one of her group, "lets ask the adjudicators if that is allowed. "No," said Amela, "one of the rules of this contest is that we do not ask the rules." After suppressing the resistance , Amela waited for the other team's member to re-enter the room, then her group lifted the table and began to move it towards the door. The opponents started kicking up a fuss when they saw that their representative could not go out into the corridor to copy the pattern, because Amela's team's table was blocking the route.

"Are they allowed to do that?", they called to the adjudicators. They received no answer. They tried again, "They're cheating," said one of the applicants, they still received no answer. "How long can they stay outside?" Each time they asked a question, getting angrier and angrier, they were met with total silence. Amela and the rest of her team sat back, started talking amongst themselves, leaving their guy in the corridor to copy the model which was easy now that he could see it all the time.

After about ten minutes, the test was called to a halt. Amela's team were the winners, this was a test for lateral thinking they were told. The next day Amela received a call at work, it was one of the adjudicators, "You have been short listed to two ," she was told, "We would like you to come to London, for a one to one interview with the Chief of our Charity. The interview went well, Amela was notified the next day that she had got the job. She had made it plain she knew very little about charities, but was assured she would have training as to the details of the disease of leprosy and the places in the world where the company did much of its work.

The following day she entered Mr. T's office handing him her week's notice, on Friday week she would be leaving his employ. He looked sadly up from the paper work on his desk, he did not say a single word. The week that followed dragged on interminably, she continued to do her work for Mr. T., but neither of them mentioned her departure which was fast approaching. At closing time on the Friday, Amela, with tears in her voice went to shake hands with her Boss, she did not speak in case she began to cry, Mr. T. stood up and extended his hand and remained silent also. It had been a good three years, she was very fond of him, and she was very sad to go, although the lure of the unknown made her anxious to do so.

As time went by, Amela visited him at his home when she heard he had been unwell. They talked about the old times, the business, Amela's new adventure and her new home. About a year or two later, she heard about Mr.T's death. Amela was very sad, and telephoned his widow with her condolences. "Is there anything I can do for you?" she asked. "Yes please," his widow replied, "Will you read the words I have written about him at the funeral which is to be held this week?" Amela consented, it would be an honour, "Mrs. T."

Amela arrived in good time at the funeral parlour, Mr. T's coffin lay in front of the chapel. She had never attended the funeral of a Jew before, but today it was not the funeral of a Jew as such, but the funeral of her former boss and friend. Family arrived from different parts of the world, friends from different parts of the U.K. and many employees who Amela recognised. The strains of Dvojak's new world symphony was being softly played as the guests arrived, Amela picked up a programme and took her seat amongst the mourners. On reading down the programme, she saw her contribution to the service was after the introduction musical piece played by Mr. T's young grandson. The item was unannounced, there was no Rabbi or Minister in the pulpit.

Amela rose to her feet and went to the pulpit. She respectfully bowed to the coffin which lay by her side. She looked at the face of Mrs. T which was bathed in sorrow, their daughter and grand children could not stop the tears from flowing down their grief stricken faces. Amela offered her condolences to the family. Before reading Mrs. T's speech, she welcomed the mourners who had come from far and wide. She introduced herself as his former employee and a great admirer of the man so few people understood.. People were invited to say a few words if they so desired, where upon several of them rose and paid their respects to the great man.

After the ceremony, the mourners went to the wake reception. Amela was unable to stay for more than a few minutes but asked permission from Mrs. T to follow the hearse to the crematorium. "I would be most grateful," she said.

The under taker respectfully told Amela that they could enter the Chapel and stay as long as they wished to say their final farewell. The strains of Dvorjak's New World Symphony were softly played while the couple stood in silence, with heads bowed before the flower covered coffin. There was no one else there to wish him good bye, the others had said their good byes at the Chapel before the wake reception. Amela will always remember him with great affection and the honour she felt to say her final words over his coffin.

Her job at the Leprosy charity was an eye opener. She had so much to learn, firstly about the logistics of a charity in general, and then the details of the disease of leprosy. She travelled to London on numerous occasions to hear lectures from historians and medical people. It was a fascinating subject. Leprosy was quite common in countries such as India, Brazil and parts of Africa. It's victims were usually poor and mal nourished. The leprosy bacteria came in two forms, attacking the nerves, particularly in the body's extremities , rendering the sufferer unable to feel their fingers, toes or parts of their faces. Because of the numbing of the nerve endings the patients, who were often barefooted, would walk on thorns or shards of stone and cut and injure their feet and feel no pain. Bacteria soon got in to these wounds, and caused the sloughing away of their toes. Their toes did not fall off, as most people assume, they were sloughed away.

In the case of the hands, patients lost the sensation of pain in the fingers, which allowed them to lift boiling pots and cans from off the fire with out feeling burns. The injuries caused were awful, the disfigurement gave the sufferer a stigma which accompanied the disease since Bible times. Although the object of the charity was to cure this disease, which was very curable , it was also their intention to remove this ancient stigma. The cost of drugs was no more than two pounds to cure one sort of leprosy and nineteen pounds to cure the more aggressive sort. It was not possible to restore the damage done by the sloughing away, the disfigurement remained with the patient till the day he died, but it was possible to arrest the disease and stop any further damage. If the disease was diagnosed in its early stages, the patient would recover without any visible signs of having had it.

The Charity had worked for many years in the country of Malawi, Africa., and had seen great progress in their aim of eradication. They had a base in south India also which was making strides to find and treat people in their poor and humble dwellings in the outlying villages and shanty towns around the big city where the office was situated. During the time of Amela's employ with the charity, their aim was to eradicate the disease off the face of the earth by the turn of the century, which had no more than twelve years to go.

Amela's office was in the centre of the large city near to where her home was. Her full time paid secretary managed the office, making appointments for the jobs that Amela had to do, and keeping in close contact with the number of volunteer committees which helped the organisation. Amela visited and addressed assemblies in almost all the schools in the North West of England. Her area extended to six counties, ie Lancashire, West Yorkshire, Greater Manchester, Merseyside, Cumbria and The Isle of Man. She also addressed Colleges, Universities, Churches, Rotary Clubs, Women's Institutes, Round Table and Siroptomists, in fact any gathering where they wanted to help in a philanthropic manner. Her objective was to raise the profile of the charity and to raise funds for the treatment of the disease.

Along with the public speaking engagements, Amela ran social events, "It's a knock out" days, or assault courses in army grounds over seen by army personnel. Sometimes she held a "Water knockout" event when she would hire local swimming centres and teams of contestants would play the games that Amela devised. All these events would be sponsored by individuals or corporate organisations and raised thousands of pounds for the purchase of drugs to treat patients.

Every month or so she would journey to Essex where the administrative centre of the charity had its offices. She would meet her colleagues, Managers who ran offices in Scotland, Somerset, Belfast, London, the North East, Devon and Cornwall and the Midlands. They shared experiences, and talked of the people who volunteered to help them in their work. They were uplifting days, days which Amela looked forward to, and remembered for a long time.

Another part of her job was to keep the Charity in the public eye, she did this by writing letters to the local newspapers in her area, approximately one hundred and twenty of them. She wrote of incidents and successes which she read about in the Charity magazine, or she would relate help and commitment she received from her volunteers and fund raisers. The public responded to these appeals with great generosity, people had sympathy for the poor and deprived victims of the disease., and either gave their time or their money to help cure it.

One Saturday evening Amela had to address a Church in Manchester. Rex , who accompanied her on most of her week end appointments, did the map reading. It was before the days of satellite navigation and the down loading of detailed instructions of route maps. After a circuitous route they arrived in the Church after the service had begun. Amela jumped out of the car leaving Rex to park up. She ran in breathlessly and caught the words of the Priest as she entered the Church "and she will be speaking on the subject of leprosy". Amela walked straight up to the pulpit . The Priest, who had never seen her before, was surprised to see this woman enter the Church and take up her position at the pulpit. It was a close call., but Amela composed herself during her greeting and continued with her message.

"If all the leprosy sufferers in the world stood with their arms outstretched and hands touching , the line of patients would encircle the globe at the equator three times." She continued with the symptoms of the disease, the congregation which ran into hundreds of people, listened intently. She informed them of the cost of treating and curing the disease, "Two pounds," she said, "Cures one sort of leprosy, and nineteen pounds cures the more aggressive strain. I will be standing at the back of the Church after the service, and would be very grateful for your donations. I thank you in anticipation."

Rex and Amela took up their positions at the entrance doors of the Church, each held a collecting box in their hands. They thankfully received the scores of donations that were put into the boxes. An old lady came up to Amela and slipped something into her hand. When Amela opened her hand to look at what the lady had put there, she was taken by surprise, it was a gold ring with five garnet stones in it.

Amela drew in her breath, "I can't take this," she said to the lady as she looked into her eyes. She instinctively felt that this ring was a gift from the lady's husband or partner, maybe a gift from her long diseased mother, but what ever it was, it was deeply sentimental and Amela did not want to deprive her of it.

"Please take it," she said, "I want you to sell it and cure one person at lease from leprosy.." Amela felt the tears of gratitude well up into her eyes. On her return to the office on the Monday, she told her secretary of the incident, "Please go into the town to one or two jewellers and have the ring valued, " Amela asked.

Amela began writing a letter to the newspapers about this incident. Her young daughter, on hearing this story, said "I'll buy the ring Mum, I'll give one pound more than any one else is prepared to give." "Please don't say that darling, some one might offer a thousand pounds for it, you can't afford to pay that much." Amela's daughter insisted. The ring was valued at twenty five pounds. The letter was printed by dozens of the news papers in the north west and donations poured in to help the cause. Many of the donations were of thirty eight pounds. No one wanted to buy the ring. After the appeal was over, Amela's daughter gave thirty nine pounds for the ring, one pound more than the biggest contribution. The old lady, by donating it had indeed cured two severely affected leprosy patients.

A year later Amela addressed the same congregation. She told them the story of the ring donation, and how much money they had raised as a result of the donation and the letter. Amela thanked every one for their support, hoping that the old lady was in the congregation to hear her gratitude.

On one of the visits to the Isle of Man, Amela organised an absail down the wall of the T.T. Grandstand. The event was to be opened by the famous comedian Norman Wisdom. One of the people taking part was a blind man. Every one stood in awe when they saw him make the descent. He had heard that blindness is another one of the results of severe leprosy, and motivated with sympathy , he raised a lot of money to help prevent this further disability in sufferers.

Amela was accompanied by her daughter during this visit. Her secretary had fixed up appointments to visit all the schools on the island, and one or two of the philanthropic organisations. On her visit to the largest school on the island, the entire school and all staff members were invited to listen to her address on leprosy. The audience numbered over one thousand pupils and staff. Amela's daughter sat some where out of view of her mother. The Head master made his announcements and introduced Amela. The pupils, who were sitting in rows on the floor to accommodate so big a crowd, were shuffling, coughing and fidgeting.

Amela rose to her feet. Picked up the microphone and whispered into it. "Can you hear me at the back of the hall, if not please would you raise your arm." The audience immediately stopped shuffling fidgeting and coughing, everyone was intent on catching every word that Amela spoke. No arms were raised. The initial impact of seeing a woman, almost six feet tall, with a brown complexion, and speaking in such perfect English was enough to silence any audience, after that Amela had to rely on her ability to tell a story with compassion and involvement.

The assembly were dismissed, Amela joined her daughter in the school yard. "That was pretty impressive Mum," she said, "You had them eating out of your hand." Amela smiled, it was the only compliment she ever received from a member of her family. What do they say, "A prophet is not without honour save in his own country and in his own home."

During the summer months, Amela's secretary booked various venues for the Knock Out events. One in each of the six counties in her area. One such booking was made in Heaton Park Manchester, which is the biggest public park in Europe. As the month of the event drew nearer, Amela was notified that a pop concert had been booked in the park for the same weekend as the Knock Out event. The promoters of the pop concert and the managers of the park assured Amela that it would be in another part of the park and would not interfere in any way with the games being held at the knock out. Amela did not accept this assurance, and negotiated a change of date for the knock out on the condition that the pop concert organisers gave her a five minute slot during the show to address the audience on the subject of the charity she represented. They agreed.

The audience they anticipated was numbering some thirty thousand people. Amela began to wonder if she had done the right thing, had she volunteered to go beyond the call of duty? She rang head office and told them of the pop concert and the crowds they were expecting, asking for advice and help from anyone who was more experienced than she was. "You're on your own Amela", she was told, "just do what you can."

She rang Flame,"Give me advice please dear Sis, how can I hold the attention of so big a crowd? The pop groups will be thundering their music over the entire park, the ground will probably be vibrating with the amplification, what can I do on my own to interest them at all?"

"You'll have to wear something dramatic Amela, some thing glittery and colourful, bounce on to the stage as if you were an entertainer."

Amela thought about it for a moment, "But all the pop groups will be doing just that Flame, I'll have to think of something different."

After some serious thought, Amela made herself an outfit. She told nobody about it, only Rex, who as usual accompanied her to the concert. On her arrival back stage Amela could feel the vibration of the music. The lights blazed into the audience, a row of heavily built bouncers stood legs akimbo facing the crowds. Group after group went onto the stage and gave their performance. Amela changed into her stage costume. When she was given her cue, she mounted the stairs onto the platform. The compare asked if she were okay, "Yes of course, " Amela answered. Her knees were knocking, Rex had gone into the audience with the video camera, it was the only time in their lives he felt nervous for her. The musicians came off the stage bringing their instruments and drum kits with them, there was a moments hesitation, Amela could hear the noisy audience, she told herself it would only be like speaking to her own children, the compare called her name.

Amela staggered on to the stage clanging a large brass bell, shouting "Unclean, Unclean, Unclean." She was dressed in a long dirty looking cloak, her hands were bandaged , her head was almost covered by a large loose fitting hood. There was no mistaking what she was dressed as. A hush came over the audience. She made her way to the microphone,"What am I going to talk to you about?" she raised her voice to the crowd. Almost as one man, the answer came back to her, "Leprosy." She'd got their attention. Teenagers and young adults, all listened intently, now their cans of beer and alcohol were second in importance in their minds. She continued with her speech, the huge crowd numbering some thirty thousand people were remarkably quiet, she concluded her speech with an appeal for their monetary help. Try as the world might, it was almost impossible to erase the old image of a person suffering from leprosy.

January the thirty first each year was World Leprosy Day. Charities who worked for the eradication of the disease and volunteer committees, along with countless scores of envelope distributors and postal donors, made a special effort to raise awareness of this disease, which was still prevalent in the poor world.. This year, the charity for which Amela worked were going to hold a service in St. Paul's Cathedral London. The Queen, who was the Patron of the charity was unable to attend due to a previous engagement, but was represented by her cousin The Duke of Gloucester. The sermon was being given by The Bishop of Malawi in whose country the charity had worked for a number of years with significant results. Present in the congregation, was The Lord Mayor of London , other V.I.P's , volunteers, interested people and of course the entire staff of the charity. Amela was asked to read the scriptures. Next to her appearance at the Pop concert , this was the most nerve racking experience of her charity working days. Her son, who was now working in The Hammersmith hospital in London and his G,P. doctor wife, and of course Rex accompanied her to the service to give her moral support. Flame and Bobbi were also present. She had given much thought to the clothes and hat she would be wearing, she designed and made a striking costume in black and white with details that only Amela would have thought of. She would probably be more nervous knowing members of her family were in the congregation.

At the point in the service when the reading from the New Testament had to be delivered, a high ranking Church official, bearing an orb in his left hand, came to where Amela was sitting and proffered his right arm ceremoniously for her to take and accompany him to the lectern .She could literally feel her knees knocking. After the slow walk to the front of the assembly , and the assent to the pulpit, Amela formally bowed to the Royal presence, The Duke of Gloucester. She commenced her delivery. The reading for today is taken from St. John's Gospel, chapter five:

"After this there was a feast of the Jews: and Jesus went up to Jerusalem.

Now there is at Jerusalem by the sheep market a pool, which is called in the Hebrew tongue Bethesda, having five porches.

In these lay a great multitude of impotent folk, of blind, halt, withered, waiting for the moving of the water.

For an angel went down at a certain season into the pool, and troubled the water: whosoever then first after the troubling of the water stepped in was made whole of what so ever disease he had.

And a certain man was there, which had an infirmity thirty and eight years.

When Jesus saw him lie, and knew that he had been now a long time in that case, he saith unto him, Wilt thou be made whole?

The impotent man answered him, Sir, I have no man, when the water is troubled , to put me into the pool: but while I am coming, another steppeth down before me.

Jesus saith unto him, Rise, take up thy bed and walk.

And immediately the man was made whole, and took up his bed and walked.

Amela added "May the Lord bless to us the reading of His Holy Word."

She rejoined her family and stifled a shuddering sigh of relief. After the service they went into the crypt for an informal presentation. Amela walked past the painting by Holman Hunt, she was reminded of the copy which hung on Lizzie's dining room wall, it was of Jesus with a crown of thorns upon his head, holding a lantern in his hand, knocking on a closed door. It read, "Behold I stand at the door and knock, if any man hear my voice and open the door , I will come in to him and sup with him. and he with me."

She was introduced to The Duke of Gloucester and several other very important people. During the champagne reception that followed, she sought the presence of Flame, Gerry's widow Bobbi, and of course, Rex, Gra and Debbie. Amela had read the scriptures countless times in many and varied Churches, but the privilege and honour to do so in the world famous St Paul's Cathedral was an occasion she would never forget.

The charity asked Amela if she would like to go on a fact finding mission to south India , to the administrative centre office near to the city of Hyderabad. She hesitated for a second and gratefully consented to their request. She had not returned to India since she left thirty seven years before. Her memories of the country were of a sheltered life in the Himalayan boarding school and an even more sheltered life at home in the central plains with the family during the winter vacation. Rex fixed his annual holiday and planned to join her after her work with the charity was over. He also bought their twenty one year old daughter an airline ticket for her coming of age present. The three of them would visit parts of the country where Amela grew up also the famous tourist sites.

The logistics of her work trip were all taken care of by the Charity. She boarded the plane which was half empty due to the first war with Iraq at the time, and the uncertainty of the safety of air space above the country. As she was approaching Delhi airport, she felt the strangest sensation in her soul. This was the land of her birth, one she had not seen for almost four decades. All her memories centred round Lizzie, "I wish you were with me Mum," she felt herself thinking. England was her home, it always had been since the day of her arrival. Being an Anglo Indian , she remembered the feeling of foreignness she felt living in a land where most people could not speak her language. The only thing foreign thing about her in England was the colour of her skin, every thing else was English, her dress, her way of life, her culture, her language, her faith, her friends and all her relations.

Amela felt alone. Not only was she unfamiliar with life as an adult in the country, but she had never been to the south, where the languages they spoke were quite different to the Hindi the servants spoke when she was growing up. She deplaned and went into the concourse of the airport. It was heaving with crowds of people, every seat was occupied, people lay huddled in blankets all over the place. Waiting one assumes for their connecting flights or the late arrivals of relatives. Amela went to the money changing booth and converted pounds to the Indian currency of rupees. She had to make her way to the domestic airport to catch a plane to the city of Hyderabad where she would be met by the charity employees.

She had been advised not to take a taxi alone but to catch a local public transport bus. It was two o'clock in the morning, she had plenty of time to connect to her next flight. She went out of the airport to the row of buses standing outside. She asked the driver of the first if he was going to the domestic airport, he said "No." She went to the second in the row, and after asking the same question, got the same answer. She continued working her way down the row. At about the tenth bus, after asking the question, a voice piped up from the back, it was one of the passengers, "Where do you want to go." he asked. "I want to go to the domestic airport," Amela said. "Just get in, "said the passenger, "he'll take you there." He then spoke to the driver in a language Amela did not understand, and nodded to her, "he will make a diversion and get you to the airport". She took her seat in front of the helpful passenger, after a few thankful words, he told Amela that he lived in Birmingham, in an Asian district, alongside thousands of immigrants that had now taken up residence in the U.K.

On her arrival at Hyderabad she was met by Jairaman, a Hindu employee with the charity. Allowing her recovery time after her long flight, she was invited to meet the rest of the staff at the office. She was told that each day they would pick her up at six thirty in the morning and take her to different areas in the outlying districts to administer the monthly dosage of drugs to patients. Some evenings they would visit villages to spread the news that the stigmatised opinion of the disease was a thing of the past and that patients should come forward for treatment which would most certainly result in a cure.

This attitude was also being helped by Princess Diana who as a patron of a sister leprosy charity was seen to be talking to and holding the hands of people with leprosy.

Other evenings, Amela would be invited to the homes of the employees to meet their families and to share their food. Every moment of this trip proved to be of great interest, whether on the road, or in the dwellings of patients and workers.

On the very first day, they drove past , what looked to Amela as a land fill refuse dump. Closer observation revealed hundreds of people and small children living in the area. Their dwelling places were covered with rusty tin sheets, scraps of plastic, rags and a host of other commodities which looked as if they had been found on the city's dumps. It was one thing to see this sort of poverty on news reels and documentaries shown on television, but quite another to be actually witnessing it at first hand.

Every one or two hours they stopped on the outskirts of a predetermined village where a group of people would be waiting for the jeep. The weather was hot. Mr. Gadenna, who was the chief medical worker and charity employee, invited Amela to accompany him and see for herself the sort of work they were doing. At each stop he would set out a small table for medical records and medication .In the back of the jeep, there would be a box with gifts which had been donated by local philanthropic organisations which had to be distributed, upon his discretion, to the most needy.

The patients had been told, on the previous visit, when their pre packed tablets had run out, they were to come to this particular spot. The time was often determined by the position of the sun, perhaps when it was overhead or in line with such and such a tree or building. The people did not have any means of telling the time, and often waited an hour or so for the arrival of the jeep, having walked across dusty, dry, arid fields. Amela was very impressed at the organisation of this drug distribution. She was so impressed at the dedication of the workers, who often went beyond the call of duty in caring and comforting the sick and needy. Some of the patients showed little signs of the disease, they had been diagnosed and treatment commenced before their fingers or toes were sloughed away, others were the most pitiful sights she had ever seen.

One day, towards the end of the distribution, Amela saw an old man , bent over double , making his way towards the voices of the charity workers. The stick which he leaned on was the gnarled and twisted branch of a tree. He hobbled up to the table for his medication. His head was bent towards the ground, he shuffled his way up to the table and stood in front of Amela. Mr Gadenna gave her the sheet of tablets to give to the old man. She touched his arm and put the tablets into his hand. She couldn't help but notice the stumps which rested on the top of the walking stick, he had lost all his fingers. Mr Gadenna then asked Amela to give him a dhothi. A dhoti is an Indian loin cloth, a pile of which had been donated by a philanthropic company for distribution to the most needy. She lifted the old man's arm slightly and placed the loin cloth under his arm. He fell to the ground and put the stumps of his hands on Amela's feet in gratitude.

"Oh, no , " she said, " you don't need to do that." Of course the old man did not understand her. Amela caught sight of his feet. To her sadness and horror she saw that he had lost most of his toes. The few that remained were twisted and deformed and crossing over in un natural positions. Amela placed her hand under his chin, raised it slightly to look at his face, to her disbelief, the old man was completely blind.

Amela felt the tears pouring down her face. She put her hands on his shoulders and raised him up. She will never forget this encounter till her dying day. That night she thought of the first time she ever saw a leper, sitting on the floor near her, at that little village hospital in central India, where she almost lost her life. Informed people do not call them "lepers" any more, they are leprosy sufferers, or patients of this most curable disease. That evening she was invited to the house of Jairaman, to eat dinner with him and his family.

On arrival, she was shown into the dining room , his mother, wife and unmarried sisters smiled shyly and stood back while the men folk in the family conversed with her. When dinner was ready, she was invited to take her place on the floor with the men , around a cloth on which banana leaves were set. The delicious food of spiced southern Indian curry and lentils was served with a variety of flat breads. The women held off eating till after the men and guest had been fed. Amela copied the others when they ate their food with the fingers of their right hands, scooping the rice and curry into little mouth sized balls and popping them into the mouth.

She noticed in one corner of this room, a small, cloth covered table with a few objects on it, a cup, a bowl, a few flowers and some sweet meats. Above the table, hanging on the dining room wall was a picture of one of the Hindu Gods. Not being familiar with the Gods, she was unable to identify him. She noticed the revered manner in which the members of the family treated that part of the room.

Day after day she accompanied the Indian charity workers to different districts. One day she went to a rehabilitation centre run by a local politician. Some forty cured leprosy patients lived there, men who had been rejected by society and family. They ran the forty acre farm on a self sufficient basis. They grew their own crops of vegetables, and tended the paddy fields. They kept goats for milk and meat, they picked fruit from the orchards they had planted. Those who had recovered without disfigurement worked in the office where they bagged up surplus grain for sale and made sandals out of old tyres for other leprosy patients.

The politician asked Amela if she would like a pair of sandals. "The workers will make you a pair." She accepted the offer gratefully, and thought they would make a very interesting talking point when she returned to her public speaking engagements in England. The shoe maker placed a piece of cardboard on the floor, round which he would pencil the outline of her foot. To her embarrassment, the cardboard was not big enough, they had to stick two pieces together. Amela wished her daughter was there to cover her embarrassment. She had always mocked the size and shape of her mother's feet, they drew round her foot, bunions and all, and said they would be ready prior to her departure from India.

At most of the distribution points, crowds gathered round the jeep and were entranced by the size of the foreign visitor. She had a brown face, but no Indian was so tall. Amela felt as if they viewed her as if she had dropped from another planet. Amela took many photographs of her visit to the rehabilitation centre. She saw a man in the paddy field, bent over, transplanting the rice shoots. He stood in about six inches of water, his hands submerged, when she caught sight of his face, she could see the disease had completely disfigured his nose.

She tried to talk to two women, Amela put her hands to her own face and made a gesture as if to request them to smile for the camera. The women did not under stand her request, they were unable to smile. However, copying Amela, they did put their hands to their faces as if to raise the corners of their lips in a smiling gesture, both of them had lost nearly all their fingers.

One day, they visited a hospital, Mr Gadenna, went from patient to patient , examining them and offering advice and consolation. He lifted the hand of a patient, the stumps of whose fingers were weeping with a bacterial white liquid. He held the man's hand in his own without any sign of the revulsion most people would naturally feel. From that moment on, Amela thought of Gadenna, as a saint. She thought too of the Christian aunt who had paid for her education, visiting Christian Churches, drawing her spotlessly white gown nearer to her as she passed beggars with leprosy, repulsed at the thought of any one touching her attire.

Steele, who knew Hyderabad very well, notified his friend Krishna, that Amela was in town, he told his friend what Amela would be doing and requested him to take her for a week end break to his own residence in a place called Bramanpalli. Amela was delighted to meet Krishna and his wife and accepted their hospitality with pleasure. He belonged to an illustrious Hindu family, whose forebears were advisors to the Nizam of Hyderabad. Krishna told Amela that his father was Justice of the Peace which sounded distant memories in her mind. As was customary, the Indian hospitality was second to none in the world. They lived in a spacious single story bungalow set in carefully tended gardens with masses of bouganvillea arching over the entrance. Amela was interested to see two arched alcoves on the dining room wall, each exhibiting a statue of a Hindu God. The other five, belonging to the set were standing on pillars outside the front veranda.

Krishna told her these were priceless objects and would fetch an amazing amount of money if they were to be sold abroad. Amela wondered why he left five of them outside knowing they were so valuable. Krishna was not worried about this, he had an armed guard standing at his main gate twenty four hours a day. Besides this, it would not be possible to obtain an export license for their foreign disposal, and they would be traced if they kept in India. He felt his religious relics were quite safe.

That evening, the Lion's Club of India were opening a hospital for the blind in the district. Since blindness is a symptom of leprosy, the charity workers were invited to attend. Many of the patients treated would be leprosy sufferers. It was to be opened by the District Commissioner who was the highest ranking official in the state. Amela had been asked, as second in the line of celebrities at this event, to make a speech. Apart from the word "Salam" which meant "greeting" she stuck to her mother tongue of English. Amela was impressed to find that many of the Indians were very good at speaking English, but in particular her friend Saint Gadenna, whose English was not only perfect but he was also fluent in seven other different languages commonly used in South India..

The next day was the last day of the two week fact finding mission after which she would join Rex and their daughter at the international airport in Delhi. Together they would continue the journey to the north of India, she would accompany them to her old school up in the Himalayas. They would then take an over night train a thousand miles into the central province of India to where her old home was. They would finally visit the famous tourist sites, and return to her beloved England. She would have so much to tell them.

As usual the jeep picked her up at six thirty in the morning. They drove out of the city to a different area. Once they had left the formally built up city suburbs, they hit another dusty red dirt tack. Amela had taken to covering her head with a scarf to keep her hair from being completely covered by red dust. This time they distributed double skinned stainless steel drinking cups which were insulated with polystyrene, the grateful recipients would now be able to hold the cup without burning their fingers, the contents of which could be a hot drink.

After the morning's work, Mr. Gadenna asked Amela if she would like to visit a Hindu Temple. "It is the birthday of our God Krishna, this week has been a holy week , devotees have come from far and wide to bathe in the pool of ceremonious cleansing and to worship our God. I know you are a Christian," he continued, "but I am still asking if you would like to come."

"Mr Gadenna, I am a Christian, there is no doubt about that, but I am also a tourist, and it would give me a wonderful experience if we could do so." She thought of the invitation to the Jewish Synagogue which Mr. T. had invited her to, but which did not materialise, she would not miss this for anything.

Across a dried up river bed, Amela could see scores of people walking barefooted toward an edifice in the distance. It was half obscured by high trees. She could just see the pointed tops of white marble which rose almost to the heavens. As the jeep drew nearer, she could see the whole wonderful temple built out of marble. The carvings and engraving on the outside held Amela spell bound. Hundreds of people were now approaching their place of pilgrimage.

After parking up, Mr Gadenna asked Amela to leave her shoes in the jeep, "We must go into this holy place with bare feet ," he said. The other members of the charity team also did the same thing. Amela took her camera bag in with her. She was shown into the office of the Chief Administrator of the temple. She sat in his office with something like twenty more officials standing around her. He explained that he would send the tourist official to accompany her round the temple, stopping at the holy booths in turn. She had a cup of tea with them, and the rest of her entourage accompanied her as she commenced her guided tour.

They walked past a vast pool of water into which the devotees would descend, fully clothed, to cleanse their sins away. Amela took a photograph of this amazing scene. Mr Gadenna asked her to hand her camera to one of the people who accompanied them . "No photographs are allowed in the temple ", he said. A bull walked slowly past her just missing her feet by inches. It was dusted with red powder. Later she learnt the bull was a vehicle of the God Krishna and was consequently revered by the Hindus. She quickly stepped out of the way. The devotees were temporarily asked to delay their acts of worship until after the visitor from England had been shown the temple.

Mr . Gadenna stayed by her side throughout this event. Being a devout Hindu, he was honoured to be treated as an escort to Amela who was to be shown what most Hindus never see in their life time. The official guide stopped at a booth. The priests, clothed in orange robes, stood in front of the booth and chanted prayers, of which Amela could not under stand a word. She not only did not understand the language, but she did not know any thing about the Hindu religion.

She was asked to cup her hands, Mr. Gadenna explaining how she was to do this, "Place your right hand into your left hand making a cup into which holy water will be poured. Then you must lift your hands to your mouth and pour the holy water slowly into your throat." Amela did not know where the water came from, and avoided it going into her mouth. It poured down her chin and onto her clothes. They repeated this operation two or three times, doing their best to ensure Amela got her share of this holy liquid. The priest put a mark in the centre of her forehead denoting she had said prayers in the temple.

They moved on to the next booth. The entourage followed closely behind her and Mr. Gadenna. She was allowed to peep into what was the Holy of Holies in the temple. She glimpsed a darkened cell with a stone sacred object inside. Mr. Gadenna explained that it was a symbol of the God Krishna. She was next shown to another passage where Lord Krishna and his revered wife were venerated. There were offerings of sweet meats and flowers placed in many places as gifts to the holy couple.

The next stop was at an open booth, she was asked to stand still and accept the cap of wisdom. A young priest, again clothed in an orange mantel, placed a fine silver cap on her head. He held the object in place whilst he chanted prayers and blessings. Mr Gadenna explained he was praying for blessing and wisdom not only for her, but for all her family, "Because we are with you," he said, "these blessings will spill over onto us as well."

Mr. Gadenna turned to the man who was carrying Amela's camera, he nodded, "Take a picture of this ." The man shook is head, "only have one left in the reel, I'm keeping that ." he replied. They moved on to what was the climax of the visit. A rug was placed on the floor and Amela was asked to sit in the middle of the rug. Beside her sat Mr. Gadenna, the rest of the party stood behind them. Two priests took their position on the rug in front of Amela. They were chanting prayers all the while. She was given some sweet meats and asked to pass them on.

The chief temple administrator sat by Amela's left hand. She passed the sweet meats to him who passed them on to the person on his left. More sweet meats were passed and more chants were sung. Then a shawl was placed on her shoulders and she was instructed by Mr. Gadenna to hold the shawl in a particular manner. Amela twisted the shawl in front of her chest, making sure it did not slip off her shoulders. When the ceremony was over, they rose to their feet and gathered in the temple garden for an official photograph. "Do you know what they did?" Mr. Gadenna asked her. "No, " answered Amela, "I only know they treated me like a princess."

"No," the answer came back, "Not like a princess Madam, but like the Head of your State, only the Queen and the Heads of nations, and our top politicians would have this honour conferred on them." Amela returned to the jeep, she put her shoes back on her feet, she was quiet, the honour of this event would not sink in until she was able to tell Rex about it.

On her arrival back at the office in Hyderabad, the workers greeted her with honour. All the Hindu employees felt blessed as a result of her experience. Word had got back to the office before the jeep did, they could not wait to hear all about this happening. Mr. Gadenna explained with pride and gratitude of the days events. "What did I do to deserve this ?" she asked. What would her grandmother Pushpa think of this honour, what would Pushpa's father Tilak think of this honour?

On her arrival back to the hotel, Amela changed into a nice dress, she had invited the Charity staff to dine with her. This was to be her treat and a small thank you for the kindness and hospitality they had shown to her during the past two weeks. The telephone rang, she was told some one was at the desk to see her. She went down to find the politician with a shoe box in his hand, "These were specially made for you Madam."

Amela expected to find the sandals made from old tyres. On opening the box she was surprised to see a beautifully hand crafted pair of leather sandals with delicate strapping which would wind round the wearer's foot and ankle. It could have been designed by a fashionable shoe designer. She thanked them profusely and returned to her hotel room to try them on. They looked enormous despite the fact they were made to look so delicate. They not only fitted Amela perfectly but enhanced her feet to their best advantage. She wore them down to dinner that night. "Wouldn't her daughter be surprised to see her mother in this delicate footwear."

The dinner went very well, they ate sumptuous fare and the bill was surprisingly low. Amela said goodbye to these wonderful people, people she would remember for the rest of her life, who were totally dedicated to treat and cure leprosy patients, it was a sad moment. She would always remember this trip as the richest two weeks in her life which she spent amongst the world's poorest people.

Chapter 13
Turn of the Century

"A bridge between east and west," the politician had said. This was an apt description not only of Amela but of all Anglo Indians. Many did not regards themselves as such, but it was just what Amela wanted to be. "A bridge between east and west."

She met Rex and their daughter at the airport in Delhi the next day. She ran into their outstretched arms, hugging and kissing both of them. "I'm so glad to be with both of you, I've felt so alone these past two weeks, although I've been with such wonderful people, I missed you enormously." She was also relieved to hear English spoken in accents she was used to.

She couldn't wait to tell them of her experiences, culminating in the exciting and honourable treatment she received at the Hindu Temple. It was a life changing experience, not in her faith, she was and always will be a devout Christian, but in the resignation and acceptance of the Hindu people to accept their lot in life, be it as a wealthy aristocrat or a poor beggar, suffering from the disease of leprosy. She did not hear one word of complaint, not one grumble or words that in English would have gone something like "WHY ME?"

She was reminded of a story she once heard.

Two men had the same dream. They dreamt they were sitting at a long dining table, laden with dishes of delicious and exquisite food. Each person sitting at the table was given a long handled spoon to use. One of the dreamers said, "It was hell, I was so hungry, starving, in fact. I could not get the food into my mouth, because the handle of the spoon was so long." The other man said, "I too had the same dream, but it was heaven, each person filled his spoon and reached across the table and fed the man sitting opposite him."

A lesson, perhaps for us all. "I cried because I had no shoes, then I met a man who had no feet."

Having completed the fact finding mission, she was anxious to show Rex and their daughter her old home, her old school, the home of her grand parents, the home in which Locky was raised. They travelled by train to Jubulpur, it was surprising to see their names written on boards outside the sleeping carriage they had reserved. The overnight journey was a new experience, for Rex and the girl. They were served dinner in their own compartment, and their berths were made up with fresh clean linen and blankets. In the morning, the bearers asked them what they would like for breakfast, the choice was between omelettes and chapattis, or a kind of watery curry with rice. The hot tea was made with milk, sugar and added spice, all boiled together.

On their arrival at Jubulpur, they were met by Locky's brother, who was now eighty years of age, and Amela's older brother. Steele who now lived in Epsom, had flown to India to meet Amela and show her the old farm and other local tourist sites. They hired a taxi and drove the sixty four miles to the town in which Locky was last Police Inspector, and to the farm where he died. The road was even worse than what Amela remembered. The ruts and holes made them hang onto each other and keep their heads tucked down for fear of bumping them on the ceiling of the car.

On arrival at the police house, memories came flooding back. Amela remembered the Christmas she spent at police lines. A large marquee had been erected in the compound, a deciduous tree had been cut down and placed in a huge terracotta pot, which was weighted down by stones to prevent the tree from toppling over. The inside of the marquee was decorated with paper chains. Tables and chairs were placed round the tent, and high up in the centre was a huge three dimensional star made from coloured crepe paper and filled with puffed rice, sugar mice and coins. Amela remembered Santa arriving in a jeep, the Christmas song "Here comes Santa Claus, here comes Santa Claus, right down Santa Clause lane," was being played loudly on a wind up gramophone. The children were screaming with excitement, presents wrapped in crepe paper were being distributed from Santa's big red sack. Lizzie stood on a chair with a big wooden spoon in her hand and broke the paper star, allowing the contents to spill all over the matting. The children scrambled round to see what they could collect, no one wanted the puffed rice, all the children went for the sugar mice, but mostly they scrambled for the money.

After this they drove to the farm. Amela was lost for words, memories of this place that went back to almost four decades filled her with nostalgia. She could see her mother standing beside the well that Locky had dug, not with his own hands but in the autocratic manner that was so characteristic of him. She looked into its thirty foot depth, she could see turtles swimming in the water. How on earth did turtles get into that well.

She wanted to show Rex the door at which she had her near fatal accident. To her surprise, the glass had never been replaced but still held the piece of hard board that was supposedly the temporary replacement for the broken pane. The mango tree was full of fruit which would ripen in the next month or so. Amela felt sad. Was it because she missed her youth or her mother, her little brother Gerry perhaps. She didn't say much, just thanked the present owners for allowing her to look at her old home. Rex could read the expression on her face, he held out his hand for her to take, and walked her slowly back to the waiting taxi.

Amela wanted to see one more thing. "Please can we drive past Napier Town, I want to see the house in which my father was raised." "Its better you remember it the way it was," Steele said, "You are going to be so disappointed if you see it." On her insistence the taxi driver w asked to drive into that part of town. A large apartment block stood in front of the Lougholme bungalow. She looked hard to see if she could see anything that resembled the Napier Town of yesteryear. She walked round to see if there was anything that remained, the super arched entrance had been knocked down to make way for the block. She was unable to glimpse any part of the lovely old bungalows that once belonged to her father's aunts and uncles.

She knew she would never go back to Jubulpur again. There was a huge hoarding at the railway station with words in bright colours printed across it, "Cleanliness is next to Godliness," it read. By the pavement at the side of the hoarding was a pile or all manner of refuse. Mangy dogs were scavenging around in the rubbish. Amela found herself longing to get back to England. India is a land of contrasts, one where extreme poverty and riches live almost side by side, and where the filth and squalor of the streets is in direct contrast to the super cleanliness of an individual.

On their arrival at Delhi, they stayed in a fabulous hotel, almost like the residence of a former rajah. Amela and her daughter dressed in glamorous clothes and jewellery and hit the tourist hot spots. The Red Fort, Fatipur Sikri, The Kutab Minar, the Bahai place of worship, the shrines of holy men, and of course the colourful market places. They shopped till they dropped to sleep at night. They walked and rode most types of transport, enjoying almost every thing they saw, almost, until they saw a beggar with leprosy. This poor man had to be carried every where by who ever was with him. His legs stopped below the knee, pointed stumps almost exposing the bones. His arms stopped at stumps below his elbows. He had no fingers or hands, all sloughed away with the ravages of the disease.

"Oh God," Amela found herself thinking, "This man has a soul like the rest of us, and you love him just the same." She resolved never to complain about her lot in life after witnessing this wretched scene.

Their final visit to tourist sites was to Agra where they visited the world famous heritage site of the Taj Mahal. It was a symbol of the love a King had for his wife who had died in child birth .Amela with her own

King Rex, walked hand in hand round the grounds before entering the sacred shrine. The workmanship and design defies description.

Before they returned to England, Amela was anxious to show her daughter and Rex the wonderful school where she had spent most of her childhood. Unlike the houses she knew in her youth, the school had changed for the better. It had been extended and improved , the newest addition to the buildings being an auditorium which seated a thousand people. Her daughter was amazed by the beauty of the mountain ranges and the setting of the buildings. Some blocks had not changed in appearance when she compared the newly taken photographs with others she had from thirty seven years before. It was here as a young teenager that Amela promised herself to take up photography, something that became her life long hobby. Is it no wonder that the internet ranks Wynberg Allen as second to none in the country, not only for its spectacular setting but for the high academic achievements of so many of its pupils.

On her return to England and her renewed work with the charity, she found a package on her desk. Amela was delighted to find a number of photographs of herself in the temple, each and every stop at booths and different situations had been photographed by the official temple photographer. Amela was completely unaware that this was happening, she only remembered the man who clicked her camera when she was sitting on the rug receiving the honoured temple shawl., so using up the last photo on her reel.

Now when she did her public speaking in schools, universities and Churches, she was able to speak with first hand knowledge. Her stories and anecdotes took on a fresh meaning. People listened in rapt attention to her experiences and the success and aim of the charity's work, much of which was a result of the generosity and dedication of the people of England.

She often smiled when she thought of Rex telling her that driving to work each day was too much for her. The distance she drove to Mr. T's firm was thirty eight miles round trip each day. The distance she covered was twenty five thousand miles per year for the charity.

The world had changed so much during the past one hundred years, it was the last decade of the twentieth century. Amela and her siblings could not forget the loss of their young brother Gerry, and often talked of Marie Louise, the American memory. The English language too had altered significantly, words were being added to and removed from the Oxford Dictionary. Words were borrowed or derived from words from other languages. The words like "bungalow", "jodhpurs", "pyjamas" and "thug", were taken from the Indian language.

Accents vary considerably, whilst the grammar might be correct, the accent often gave away the area or the country of one's origin. Second generation Caribbean, Indian , Pakistani or Chinese people speak with no accent. So many television reporters have perfect English accents, and one has to look at them to know from which part of the world their parents originated.

The major countries of the world now spoke English as their mother tongue and many others as their second language. It was the language of the air, every pilot and air crew were instructed from the ground in English , it did not matter if the plane they were flying belonged to Russia , China or India. The exception to this universal corporation or event was The Olympics. The first language of which is French, the reason being the commencement of the new Olympics was staged in Paris, some time during the last decade of the previous century.

Ruth May was performing in an open air concert in Melbourne , Australia. The amphitheatre was equipped with powerful loudspeakers. She took up her position on the podium. With knees knocking, she lifted her voice and began to sing the song best associated with her.

"I saw a peaceful old valley"………she continued.

Unbeknown to her, in the audience was an Australian man whose wife had died some years before. He had never considered re-marriage. He felt the strangest sensation come over him. He looked at Ruth May in total admiration. She concluded her song in her powerful manner:

*"And I heard a voice within me thunder,
This is worth fighting for."*

Ruth May, who was now in her sixties met the man after the concert. Denis, got to know her during the weeks and months that followed. He became her friend and lover and much to the delight of her siblings in the U.K , she became his wife. He was a typical Australian, friendly and down to earth, no airs and graces about this man. He adored Ruth May, and she him. Many of her associates and former relatives disapproved of the union until they met Denis. He was "Charm" personified, as they got to know him, they too were enchanted. All his new relations loved him for making Ruth May so happy.

Amela, received a telephone call from Flame. "I've just had a diagnosis of my illness ,"she said, "I have cancer of the throat and tongue." Amela fell silent, Flame began to cry. "They do not think they can do much for me, they cannot operate, I will not give them permission to do so, so they are going to give me a course of chemo therapy and radiation. If this fails," she said, "I'm going to die Amela."

The months that followed were peppered with sadness and joy. Flame was going to be a grandmother in November, and Amela was going to be a grandmother for the fourth time in December. Every day during that spring Amela rang her sister in London for an update of her condition and to give her moral support during the chemo treatment. One day she was hopeful, but the hope was dashed when the sickness followed.

In the August of that year , Amela's doctor daughter in law gave birth to her first child, a lovely little girl whose Welsh name was given her after her maternal grand father's nationality. Flame was admitted into a hospice when they found her condition to be terminal. Her own daughter in law gave birth to a lovely baby girl towards the end of November. When the baby was three days old, they took her to see her grandmother in the hospice. Flame could hardly breathe, the tumour had grown so much that it was almost blocking her air ways. She wanted the door of her ground floor room to remain open to allow air to get to her. It was cold and foggy, she wrapped the baby in the shawl that Ruth

May had sent her from Australia, and held her to her aching heart. They named the baby Skye, her grand mother will always be reflected in that child. The only photo of Flame and the baby was taken at this time. Amela was needed in Canada to look after her eighteen month old grand son while her Canadian daughter in law gave birth to another baby. She travelled to London to visit Flame in the hospice prior to her flight to Canada. She sat on the bed and took Flame's foot in her hand. Her sister had always laughed about the corns and bunions on her feet, they were twisted with the constant use of high heeled pointed toe shoes.

"You have beautiful feet," Amela said, choking back the tears. She did not see the corns or the bunions but only remembered the tender care her sister had shown her since she was a little girl. She remembered the time in School when she bit Flame on the hand only to have her sister lie on her behalf to save her from a good hiding. They hardly spoke, both knowing this was the last time they would be together. She thought of the tragedy that Flame had suffered when her first born son died of meningitis whilst on his honeymoon in India. She reflected sadly on the break down of her marriage. Her first husband Peter had been to visit her, he told her he always thought she was beautiful and that he would always love her. Flame was finding great difficulty in speaking. She was unable to eat and drink and refused to have a feed placed directly into her stomach to nourish her. ."Bye bye darling, " Amela said, "I'll see you soon." She left the room allowing Jim to spend a few minutes alone with his dying wife.

Amela sat in the corridor crying her heart out, waiting for Jim to come out and take her to the airport. A few minutes later he came and pressed a bunch of tissues into Amela's hand. "Why did you do that Jim?" Amela asked.

"Do what?" he asked, "That," Amela answered showing him the tissues. "Oh," he said, "I was leaving the room when she asked me to give you the tissues, she said you would be needing them and knowing you, you would not have a hanky with you." She did not let Flame see her crying. But Flame knew that her sister's heart was breaking and she was trying to be brave and not upset her with her tears.

A few days later when Amela was in Canada, the telephone call came informing her of her sister's death. "Do you want to go back to England for her funeral," her son asked her. "No, darling," she told him, "I have a job to do here which I cannot miss."

Flame was buried on the same day as Amela's grand son was born.

Amela retired from her job with the charity. As the last decade of the twentieth century drew towards its end, more grandchildren were born to her and Rex. They were happy and content in their retirement, helping when ever and where ever they could with the little ones. The grand children ranged in colour from alabaster white with jet black hair to golden summer tans with auburn and blonde hair. People were often amused when they saw Amela with them, not believing they could be her grand children. One thing they all had in common however, was their stunning good looks..

Chapter 14
Millennium

John William had been disinherited, his family home given over to the Heritage because the illustrious family had no more living descendants. Hanging on the dining room wall., in a little hamlet called Vessey in Normandy, France, was a copy of the picture of the ninety year old gentleman. Below him is a picture of his daughter Lizzie, sitting alongside a handsome gentleman in police uniform, his strong hand resting on a topee.

Below this pair, hangs a row of photographs of their eight children, all taken in their youth. Someone was once heard to say, "They all look like film stars." Steele, Ruth May, Beatson, Marie Louise, Alston, Flame, Amela and Gerry. The picture of Amela was taken in a studio when she first arrived in England. She was sixteen. Written in the corner, barely visible, are the words "With love from the original," the photo was given to a man who became her life long mate.

It was the turn of the century, Queen Elizabeth 11 had been on the throne of Britain for almost fifty years. No more could it be said, "The British Empire was the empire on which the sun never set." Many countries who were ruled by the Empire now had independence and self rule. The world had shrunk considerably - it was easy now a days to traverse the length and breadth of land and sea,. to any point on the compass, for the purpose of business, permanent dwelling or a temporary commercial base.

Second homes became very popular to vast numbers of people of the richer nations. People were earning huge sums of money due to the modern technology and satelite communication. The richer nations, by definition - the likes of U.S.A, Canada, Japan, China, Germany, France, Australia, to mention but a few - but for the purpose of this personal historical novel - are India and England.

News of natural disasters and wars spread instantly across the world, thanks to the satelite . It was possible to talk to anyone of your choosing wherever they might be - an isolated farm in central India, or a densely wooded jungle in the foot hills of the Himalayas, or whilst travelling at great speed in a vehicle which carried arms to war. Nothing was hidden from the eye of the camera. Spectacular footage showed the workings and habitats of underwater creatures and almost extinct animals and myriads of species of insects. Animals, whose habits and habitats revolved were in minus fifty degrees and plus fifty degree temperatures, were miraculously photographed.

Completely dark caves where light never penetrated housed bats before not known to humans. Take the incredible bat, what can one say about the bat? The writer often likens the Anglo Indian to the bat, neither mammal or bird. Both suckle their young, and so are mammals, birds fly and so do bats, does that make a bat a bird?

The year is two thousand. International travel became a "Must" to millions of people. Summer holidays and winter sports became adventures that people looked forward to all year round. Gone are the days when skis were the width and shape of floor boards and was once the pass time of only the rich and famous. It was now within the reach of so many enthusiasts, thanks to the budget airlines.

What changes had this century seen? Possibly more in the past one hundred years than all history put together. Good education no longer meant a nine month trip to a school a thousand miles away from home. It did not rely on a private tutor who cost a fortune. All you had to do was to log onto the internet for all kinds of information.

One could research the net for enclosure laws, famous Anglo Indians, the Hindu Caste system or historical figure such as Mahatma Gandhi

One could research historical events such as the clean air act, the war in the Suez Canal, or the prestigious standing of your school, be it in Yorkshire, Ontario or India. You could learn about any religion you wanted to, any creeds, any songs, any poems. Gone are the days when Bibles were smuggled into countries, where it was impossible to obtain literature or preach openly without risking your life. For example, log onto the website of Stewarton Bible School 777 and apart from a vast number of Christian doctrinal teachings of yet unexpounded prophecies, you will find outlines of inter denominational sermon material and the entire King James Version of the Bible.

The Anglo Indian youth, who began to study the Good Book on a forty acre farm some fifty years ago, is responsible for putting more on the net than the great Scripture Union, The Roman Catholic Church , or , come to that, any other body of Christian people in the world. Even the BBC point to his website for further information. How did he do this? He was not of the internet generation. Ironically, he worked for the largest bank in the world, at the advanced age of fifty years, they sent him on a computer course to London.

"The computer language is so different from anything I know" he once said to Amela, "Its like boarding a train at full speed while it is running through the station."

Oh, he mastered it alright - astonishingly.

Commuting became a common word in the English language. Commuting on a daily basis from ones home in the country side to the cities in the land. Commuting on a weekly basis to the great cities of the world. Commuting, albeit, in a more leisurely manner to one's holiday home several times a year. It was the year two thousand.

Lizzie would have been one hundred years old this month. She had been dead for thirty seven years. It was easy to calculate her age, she was born in the year nineteen hundred.

So many changes, not only in the world, but in her own family. How would she have felt, had she seen her own children and grand children achieving what she could never have dreamed about. Among her children, listed on the internet, under the heading FAMOUS ANGLO INDIANS -

Gerry, musician and poet, born Gerald Cranston Frederick Loughran,

Loughran I.S. Commander of the 37th Fighter Squadron, Indian Air force,

Beatson with his detailed internet site, and

Amela a Justice of the Peace.

Amongst her grandchildren,

Women who had attained the highest level in the world's stock markets .

A consultant Physician and Gastroentrologist, a writer of text books, translated from English to Chinese, to be found in most libraries in the world, one who served in the same hospital as she did, she as an orderly and her grand son as a Senior Registrar. This grandson who now represents the North west of England in conferences on the subject of intestines and stomachs.

Other grand children who were company directors, grand daughters who were high in the nursing profession, one who master minded a number of health care homes in Germany.

An ethics consultant, a grandson who is arguably the best in Canada, who is commissioned to write the ethics for 2010 winter Olympics to be held in Vancouver. .

Another grandson who is the sound recordist for the famous Harry Potter films.

A young, caring, trusted child minder registered as a special needs carer, never once mixing her own mother hood and minding skills, a pillar of her village society in the scenic county of West Yorkshire of England.

There were others of course, highly educated people in technical design, in multi language occupation, speaking Spanish and French as if it were their native tongue, and of course her millionaire grandson.

It was the turn of the century, the new millennium, what better time to have a Loughran-Cranston reunion, it was twenty years since the last one, held at the farm house on the Pennines in England. That time when they all got together to welcome their sister Ruth May whom they hadn't seen for almost three decades. It would be so different now. Sadly, Flame and Gerry had both died, they had completely lost touch with Marie Louise and her family in U.S.A., and Ruth May who had recently re-married the wonderful Australian guy would not be coming but would send her eldest daughter to represent her.

This time invitations were sent to all members of the Loughran Cranston family, it was to be held in a farm house belonging to Rex and Amela and was situated in the rolling planes of Normandy France. It was an ancient house built in 1843 which Rex and Amela had renovated, converting the cow shed and the stable into another two houses. It was built of stone and had granite coynes around the windows and doors. Rex and Amela had fallen in love with the house the moment they stepped out of the estate agent's car.

"Do you like it? Rex asked Amela.

"Yes, I do" she replied, "Do you?"

"I do too," "We'll have it," Rex told the agent.

"You cant do that", the agent said, "You haven't even seen the inside."

"Oh, don't worry about that", Rex replied, "We'll renovate the inside." The building rose three stories up in the middle, with the cow shed on one side and the stable on the other, in all it measured about eight five feet across and looked imposing. The field behind the house was full of thistles but the couple were not daunted. Inside the floors were earth, no concrete or paving, no toilet, water or electricity. No floors to the upstairs, in fact, no stairs, except for a rickety old ladder.

The place had been empty for fifteen years and had been previously owned by an aged spinster. You could look right up into the heavens where the roof tiles were missing. Very nice when they first saw it, because the sun was shining and the sky was blue.

They bought the place and set to to renovate it bit by bit, there was no urgency and every thing was a hobby as far as Rex and Amela could see. When finally the main buildings were completed, they decided to invite every one to a re-union to replicate the fabulous nineteen eighty "Do."

Family arrived from as far a field as Australia, Canada, U.S.A. Germany, Scotland and England. Locky's eighty year old brother, the only survivor of that generation, was too old to make the journey from India. Lizzie's sister Florence had died years before, but was represented by her daughter Felicity, one from the former Cranston family, she was John Williams grand daughter. Felicity was a successful interior home designer, and lived in the south of England.

Lizzie's sister Alice, who had been dead for a very long time was represented by her daughter Evelyn from the U.S.A. Evelyn was somewhere in her middle seventies. Of Lizzie's descendants there were representatives from all eight of her children .

Beatson had been ill a few years before. He'd had a heart attack and a triple bypass operation, some days he felt good, others he felt weak and lifeless, but was not going to miss this reunion for anything in the world.

His children drove down from Scotland to Normandy, each in their own cars, his eldest daughter drove to France from Bavaria. The youngest daughter brought her new born baby all the way by car from Scotland. She had given birth to her first child only three weeks before, there were parts of her body that hurt when she sat for any length of time, but despite the discomfort she seated herself on an air cushion and made the thousand mile journey. As for Beatson, his wife Inge brought him from Glasgow to Portsmouth by train.

They had to change in London, where she pushed the wheel chair, running where even she could with a large suitcase, balancing on Beatson's lap, they caught the connecting train to Portsmouth, with twenty seconds to spare. Rex and Amela met them at Portsmouth and they caught the ferry together to Normandy.

Amongst the guests was Alston's wife Rea. She had rounded up the members of the family who could get away from their places of work

The Dining Room Wall

Her millionaire son and many of her grand children were there, ranging from Gemma the teenage language expert to little Bradley and seven year old Natasha.

The flags of the nine nations represented were hung all over the place. A programme of the catering and entertainment details hung on the Dining Room Wall for all to see. Each evening a different family was responsible for entertaining or catering. There were fifty seven people there, some slept away in other gites and houses, most slept at Vessey.

Hundreds of photographs were being taken, little digital cameras almost falling out of every pocket at the celebrations. Any one who could play an instrument and was able to transport it easily, banded together to make a mini orchestra.

The music was heavenly. Amongst the players was a violinist who had previously entered the young musician of the year contest in Britain, she was playing Locky's violin. Her father Beatson picked up a guitar, he who had never had a music lesson in his life, but became a self taught music teacher, with deep, deep emotion looked into the eyes of his wife Inge and sang the beautiful words of the song,

> *Have I told you lately that I love you,*
> *Have I you told you once again some how,*
> *Have I said with all my heart and soul how I adore you,*
> *Well darling I'm telling you now"* .They had been married forty four years. Truly a union made in heaven.

Gerry's widow started to cry, her husband had died when he was so young. She missed him enormously, they had been so happy together and at the early age of forty five he had gone. His music rang round the farmhouse all through the days, his rich adept guitar playing, that made him one of the best guitarists in the world. No one was there to sing like Ruth May . Her eldest daughter had flown in especially from Australia. She did not have the power and tone of her mother's voice, but with rhythm .and bounce she gave a rendition of the Aussie song "Waltzing Matilda, Waltzing Matilda, who'll come a waltzing Matilda with me". Every one missed Ruth May, but applauded Genny with love and humour.

Rea organised a huge family meal of chilli concaney cooking in several pots in all three kitchens and then mixing the whole lot together - it tasted fabulous.

Song books compiled by Loughran,Loughran and Loughran containing family favourites were handed out, songs that Locky and Lizzie used to sing ,

> "Little pal when Daddy's gone away
> Promise you'll be good from day to day,
> Do as mother says and never sin
> Be the man your daddy might have been
> Daddy never had an easy start,
> So this is the prayer that fills my heart,
> I want you to be, little pal,
> What your daddy couldn't be, little pal,
> I want you to laugh and to sing and to play,
> To look after mother when daddy is away,
> I'll pray day and night, little pal
> That you'll turn out right, little pal,
> And should you ever be on a new daddy's knee
> Don't forget about me, little pal".

There wasn't a dry eye in the place, memories stirred and hearts remembered.

Unlike nineteen eighty, when only the siblings remembered, where there was no place for Rex, Inge, Rea or paradise girl, this time they all remembered. They were truly descendants of John William Cranston and Jacob Beatson Loughran, descendants who had left India and scattered all around the world, and were reunited to celebrate the turn of the century, and the end of an era.

At the end of the week every one returned to their own homes, in Australia, Canada, Germany, Scotland and England. Amela's son was the last to leave, he stayed on to help Rex and Amela clear up the farm house and put away souvenirs which would be handed down to future generations.

The telephone rang - Amela's son answered it. He solemnly replaced the receiver and went in search of his mother who was cutting the lawn. "What's the matter darling?" Amela said, " you look so solemn?" He put his arm round his mother's shoulders, and could barely keep the tears from choking what he was going to say.

"I'm so sorry Mum", he said, "I'm so so sorry, I've just had a phone call from Scotland, your brother Beatson is dead".

"No, it can't be" Amela whispered, "It can't be, he's only just left us" "Please tell me it's not true son."

"Come back to the house and speak to Aunty Inge, she'll want to talk to you" Amela got off her mower and could hardly make her way to the house. She knew her son would not have said such a thing if it were not true. The shock was too much for her, she could not cry in disbelief.

"Hello Inge, " Amela said, "What's happened?"

"Beatson died this morning," she said, "it was such a shock, last night we went to a wedding reception, and we were dancing with each other," she went on, "this morning ,I got up and went to prepare lunch because the family were all coming after the Sabbath service. I went to tell him to come down stairs, breakfast is almost ready" she continued. Amela was silent. Beatson was still in bed, "What's the matter? " I asked him. "Nothing " was his reply, "I just feel a little tired, let me look at you one more time my darling, you're so beautiful". I told him not to hurry, to stay in bed this morning, I'd go to Sabbath service on my own."

"I came downstairs, and within ten minutes, he followed me", Inge continued "I went into the dining room as I heard his footsteps, are you alright darling? He took a couple of steps and I caught him as he collapsed, and I seated him in a chair."

"Just then the girls came in to take us to Church, Beccy opened his shirt and Esther started giving him respiratory help. I told them to let him be, Amela, I knew he was dead."

She started weeping bitterly. "The paramedics arrived in minutes, but his time on earth was over, God wanted him, his work on earth was done."

"I'll catch the next ferry over to England, and I'll be up to Scotland as soon as I can." Beatson and Inge had been married forty four years.

The funeral in Scotland was an event not to be forgotten. It was a warm summer's day. The streets in his town had been closed as a mark of respect. Beatson had been a town councillor and all the local councillors waited amongst the hundreds of others in the local Church of Scotland.

Inge and her children walked behind the hearse. Steele. Alston and Amela followed them, then row upon row of mourners, old people, neighbours, little children, friends and many more relations.

The funeral obituary was read by Rex. It went something like this:

"Forty four years ago today, at this very time, I was standing at the head of the Church waiting for Beatson to bring me my bride. We shared our lives with him, culminating in the most wonderful week in France. Thank you Inge for making the sterling effort of bringing him there, battling long train and ferry rides, crowds of people and always coming through with a smile on your faces. Our children have grown up together, one in spirit and family, although many miles away from each other in homes scattered through out the world."

Inge read a poem that Beaton had written decades before, it went something like this, "And now to end it all, I am with God."

His children and siblings lowered the coffin into the grave, after which, every one went to a country house hotel for the wake. A lone piper played "Amazing Grace", from his stand on the tiered terraces. This was truly a celebration of a Man of God's life."

Amela took the picture of herself and Beatson to the country house. It was taken just prior to their entry into the Pentecostal Chapel when Beatson was giving her to Rex as his bride. Her veil still covered her face. Beatson looked so handsome and happy, he had been married two weeks prior to Amela's wedding. Today another photo was taken, his widow and their four children. Who would have expected this weeks ago? He is dead. Beatson is dead, but thanks to the internet, he yet speaketh.

Very soon after this sad event, Rex and Amela bought a field adjoining their French place .They started turning it into a memorial garden, it was a quagmire filled with ferns, dock leaves and thistles. Systematically they turned each section of it into an acre of memorial plants and pools filled with fishes. In the centre of a perfect English lawn they planted a specimen tree. At the new entrance into the memorial garden, they planted a weeping Cedar tree, a gift from Beatson's widow Inge. She painted words on a heart shaped granite stone, which read, "Precious in the eyes of the Lord is the death of his saints".

Four of her eight precious siblings were dead.

Amela never forgot the wonderful people and times they'd had. Gerry's widow and sons gave Amela an ornamental cherry tree, under which a guitar shaped notice bears his name. A fabulous white wisteria, with prize winning blooms, reminds Amela of her sister Marie Louise whose wedding dress she borrowed. And who could forget Flame, an antique bench bearing her name reminds Amela constantly of her precious sister. It stands beside a pool filled with water lilies and fish.

Amela spends precious quiet moments here, thinking and dreaming of times past. She still feels angry and resentful that Flame left her so young in life. Now when Amela had so many grand children, how she would have loved to spend time with her sister. Do things become more precious when they are past. Yes ! Yes! I think so. Amela felt old, so unlike her vivacious, enthusiastic , happy, youthful personality. Amela felt old.

They continued to work in Normandy on their garden and home, some how things became more and more difficult to do. Amela, philosophical by nature, often thought about youth. What? She would ask her friends is the main characteristic of youth. The answers she got back were many and varied. Its energy. Its speed, its career chasing, its finding romance and love - its enthusiasm. Yes that is what Amela felt. Its enthusiasm, that gives a person the main characteristic of youth, enthusiasm in whatever one wanted to do.

Rex became slower and slower in do- it- yourself projects, and lumbered about almost dragging his body with a reluctance that did not make Amela happy. She'd often go and do things on her own, visit her widowed sister in law in Scotland, take a trip to Canada to look after the grandchildren, go on a shopping spree with their daughter or visit the new ski chalet their Doctor son had bought in the French Alps.

One day Rex realised he could no longer go upstairs to bed, or even to walk across the room without shuffling his feet. He was unable to lift one foot at a time without excruciating pain crippling his lower spine. Rex had had cancer of the prostate gland some 15 years before and Amela was convinced this was a recurrence of that dreaded disease and that he would soon be in a wheelchair. She'd heard of people who had been confined to a wheel chair and had died within three months of the diagnosis.

She drove him to the doctor's surgery where an appointment was made for him to see a consultant. Amela was beside herself with worry, but did not let Rex see her in this state. She telephoned their son and told him of Rex's pain. When he came to visit his dad, he immediately went upstairs and packed a case to take him to the hospital. "I'll take you in Dad" said their son.

It was pathetic to see how a strong, energetic, hard-working man could be cut down so low. They helped him into the hospital waiting room. Amela lay her head on Rex's shoulder while their son went to park the car, on his return Amela could see tears in his eyes. He said nothing, just looked sadly at his suffering father. He explained to the doctor in charge how he, as a consultant physician himself would like to see his father admitted into hospital. "He is unable to manage at home, the stairs, or even to walk across the room without severe pain in his lower spine.

"We'll do what we can," they said in the hospital, "we'll run all the tests possible and treat him, if we can, to ease the pain"

Amela and her son left the hospital. The next few weeks dragged on interminably. Each day Amela would visit Rex and sit beside his bed holding his tired hand, carefully avoiding the needles and drips that were stuck in him.

The doctors all gathered round his bed, was it this or that? More tests, more blood taken, more drips, more medication - poor Rex - he lay motionless for most of the time. Each day he went down to have x rays and more tests. The colour drained away from his otherwise ruddy face and hands, he looked ghostly pale - and lifeless.

"Oh God, please dear God, don't let him suffer so", Amela prayed.

Almost three weeks later, a senior consultant stood by his bedside. "I think we've found the cause of the trouble Rex" he said. "It is definitely not a recurrence of the cancer, I think you have an abscess on your pelvic bone, it is very rare indeed, in my thirty or so years as a doctor, I have only come across it twice before. I'm going to treat you with very strong medication for six months, hopefully that will do the trick."

Rex couldn't wait to tell Amela and the children of the outcome of his weeks in hospital. When they were satisfied that they were right, the doctors discharged him. Amela brought him home and wrapped him in the proverbial cotton wool. She did not want to live if he should die, she'd much rather have him in a wheel chair at home , than for her to live any where in the world without him.

"Lets put the house up for sale and move to a smaller single storied house", she said, "one nearer the children in case we should need care" "Lets also sell the French house" he replied, "It looks like we're not going to be able to travel there any more, let alone be able to tend the acres of gardens and the houses.

The months that followed were very unhappy - it was ages before Rex got any colour back in his face and hands. He moved about as best he could, and because of his optimistic nature he assured Amela he would not be dying, not yet anyway.

Their three children were a great source of comfort to them. They phoned almost on a daily basis, from Merseyside, from West Yorkshire and from Canada, their friends and family were all supportive, which made Amela feel she was not alone in bearing this sadness. Amela was very busy taking care and helping with the grandchildren. Before long,

Rex began to read and play with them again. He lay out a train track in his workshop and had small tools for the little boys to play with when they came over. He told them wonderful stories, all made up about a friendly ghost called George. The children listened intently as their parents had done before them.

Rex was a wonderful father, present at the birth of all three of his children. He was an excellent grandfather, teaching them and reading to them for hours on end. Rex was a wonderful husband ,re-phrase, a good husband. Amela often remembered the time when Flame came to visit her during her lunch hour at Air Pumps - how intent and sure she was she'd cut Amela out and get Rex to fall in love with her, it didn't happen of course. Rex had agreed she was pretty, "but not as pretty as you Amela", he had said.

All through the decades of their marriage, it had been the same. He quite literally had eyes for no one else. He always regarded Amela as beautiful, with a perfect figure. "Love is blind," they say, and Amela was glad this was true.

As the months and years went by, Rex regained a lot of his old strength. His joints still ached with the onset of arthritis, but he battled against it and kept up with his numerous do-it-yourself hobbies. He'd spend hours in the garden and took up a full time job in his favourite place in the home - the kitchen.

He did almost all the cooking, wading through his recipe books and placing delicious meals in front of his queen. He truly was the King of his castle, and never more at home than when he turned the fire on and drew the curtains, so shutting the world out, and he and Amela were alone.

When the weather improved, they'd go to their French residence in Normandy, where, by now, they'd made some very good friends, British and French. During the summer holiday season visitors from all over the world would arrive and rent their homes for a week or two, thus providing a new and added interest to their happy lives.

Chapter 15
Golden conclusion

The year is 2006.

"Rex" Amela said, "we've been together for fifty years, surviving through ups and downs, do you think we have reason to celebrate this golden anniversary?"

"Yes, I think we do Tops", that is the name he gave to Amela when they were first married, and it had stuck now for 5 decades. "What do you think we should do?"

They discussed various possibilities, a trip to India, a weekend in Prague, a visit with the kids to London or Paris, a posh dinner in a swanky restaurant. They remembered their fortieth wedding anniversary, which Amela often says was the happiest day in her life. The children had prepared a surprise party for them inviting all their friends from all over Britain, even their son from Canada arrived unbeknown to the honoured pair. It was magic, how on earth they kept that secret, Amela could never begin to imagine.

"No Rex, lets have a great big party in France, this time it wont be a re-union of the Cranston-Loughran family, it will be our party, yours and mine and we'll invite all our friends and of course all the family too." We have so much to be thankful for."

By now Rex was becoming proficient on the computer and he set to, in the early part of the year 2006 preparing invitations. He removed their wedding photo from their dining room wall and scanned it into the computer, beside it he placed the head of a bewigged judge, and the words "you have been sentenced to fifty years of hard labour and only released when you are called from above." Inside he stated the venue and the dates for the celebrations. It was received by dozens of family and friends with humour. "Trust them" was the general comment. The replies of acceptance poured in for weeks and weeks after, those who could not make it to France were invited to their Son and daughter-in-laws place in Merseyside the following month, the place where their fortieth anniversary surprise party was held.

Greeting cards poured in by the score as the date of the great celebration drew near. Inge arrived from Scotland, it was a poignant visit, had Beatson not died six years before, they too would have been celebrating their golden wedding.

The partying went on for five days, each evening an average of fifty guests arrived, b.b.qs and scrumptious salads being served, followed by a very English trifle dessert. Wine flowed like water. Rex and Amela thanked God for all this happiness.

Their children, and eight of their nine grand children were present, unfortunately, the eldest, a girl of twenty two years of age was unable to get time off from her work and studies.

A friend gave them a photograph album especially to record messages and photos of this glorious week, something for them to keep forever, something for them to show others of the unconventional way they celebrated a golden wedding.

Guests flew in from Canada, Australia, Lancashire, they drove in from Scotland, Kent, from West Yorkshire, Merseyside and other parts of the British Isles. Rex and Amela took the opportunity to thank their friend , the plasterer John for all the work he had done to convert the cowshed and the stable into such fabulous places.

John was their Guest of Honour.

It was with pride and gratitude that Amela showed every one round the gardens. So many people had given them plants and had helped over the years in lawn cutting and pruning.

Do you know anyone who is as happy as they are? Their lives have been full of interest and joyous events, and they are sublimely conscious of these blessings. Please do not be dismayed reading of their happy lives, when yours may be lacking in true joy. There were times when they would have split, when things did not go according to plan, when promises given were broken, and hearts injured. But that was over, they still rowed and screamed at each other, but that too soon passed and they remembered and were grateful.

2006. The previous re-union was in 2000 and the first one in 1980.

They walked round the garden together. Every one had gone home. Beatson's tree was outgrowing the corner spot by the gate. They would have to remove some other plants around it so giving it more space to spread its wide and sweeping branches.

Gerry's tree was about ten feet tall now and needed pruning and thinning out, and as for Marie Louise's wisteria! - If you know anything about wisteria, you'd know it could grow around eighteen inches in a week, sending out tendrils and enveloping anything that was near by. Flame's bench was the same as always, blue and gold and a constant reminder of Amela's fabulous sister.

Amela still kept the last card that Flame had sent to her, it read "Dear Amela, thanks for being such a wonderful sister and friend. Our stay with you made us closer than ever before, and Jim and I thank you . for having us. We love you and hope you have a great day" Flame had died in 1994, ten days after her granddaughter Skye was born and twelve years before this celebration, but had she been alive, she would have been there and her wishes would have been the same.

Gerry can still be heard on c.d's which are available on his website "http://www.gerrylockran.com/" The song that Amela particularly likes is the one he wrote about Lizzie. "She was a very good friend of mine"

They returned home after a very hectic summer. It rained a lot in Lancashire, hence the lush and green pastures, food for scores of grazing sheep and lambs and of course cows that provided gallons of milk.

Amela and Rex unpacked the car, placing all the lovely gifts they were given in appropriate places. She came across the album and started carefully looking again at the wishes inside. Some of the words made Amela laugh. Their young son had written, in French, "Thank you for making me." Amela had commented beside it, in English, "It was a pleasure darling."

The book was full of photos of their fancy dress night and the football match they played on the local pitch, England versus the rest of the world, such a terrific week and one which they will never forget. But there is one entry that was written that they'd like to share with you, it reads:-

"How does one write a letter to one's parents?

First, which ever way you slice it, fifty years, a half century, is a magnificent achievement. Dogged determination, a stubborn refusal to let go, perhaps - but I'd say love, a great, wonderful, enduring, exemplary love. Some would say, your work was complete, more or less, on your wedding night - after all I'm the one writing, but there is of course far more.

I'll stick with love, but your examples of love, yes for each other and yes of course for your children and grandchildren are examples to trumpet, celebrate and emulate. But still your work is not done, there will be more examples to set to family and friends, more things to build, and many. many things to show and share with kids and grandkids.

And one more thing, your strength and power, passion and energy are obvious and legendary, let me add one more thing, be gentle with each other. You have both been gentle with me, with my mistakes and foibles, and frankly that feels wonderful. Be gentle with each other. I love you. R.

Amela closed the album and placed it with the dozens of others on the book shelf in the dining room. She had been an avid collector of photos all her life and probably had in excess of ten thousand in her library. Each album was carefully put together and every picture had details and explanation written beside it. They were bequeathed to her children and her grandchildren, selecting each child if the majority of photos in that book told of their lives.

Amela felt low. She gazed for the millionth time at the spectacular scenery in which her home is set, never failing to admire it. Beyond the verdant meadows that come right up to the back garden wall are hills and valleys dotted about with white and stone built cottages. The nearest neighbour is a pub sited at the far end of the field.

Far in the distance you can see a range of hills of which the highest is Pendle. Pendle has the reputation of being the last place in Britain where witches practised, were subsequently tried and hung. The mystery that surrounds this historic place brings scores of tourists and sight seers from all over the world, hundreds of who are seen walking to and from the summit, clad in their mountain boots and rain coats and wielding canes of various descriptions.

Some time during the early part of the nineteenth century, the enclosure act permitted people in Britain to buy parcels of land from the government for purposes of farming, mining, weaving and manufacture. Separating each parcel of land was a thirty foot strip marked by hedges or stone walls flanked by pastures, meadows and works entrances. The thirty foot strip provided passage for horse drawn carriages and hay wagons to access the fields and carry produce to and from barns and places of work.

On the corner of one such parcel of land stood a large imposing stone building, for the one part a barn, and the other a beer house with family accommodation. The owners supplied beer and a simple hot mid-day meal to the dozen or so men who worked at the near by colliery.

In those days it was usual for a man and wife to serve at the beer house whilst the older children would walk to mills and factories, sometimes close, but more often than not, miles away, to earn a small wage which would help to raise the younger members of the family.

The beer house was built in eighteen forty three, sited at the corner of the greenest field you ever did see. Today it is rendered and painted a brilliant white. The large, imposing black door stands between two stone doorposts, on the top of which and supporting the arched lintel are shaped stone decorations, resembling that of a Corinthian arch. The door has big brass fittings, the whole thing makes a very impressive entrance.

On opening the door one is greeted by the welcoming smell of a Lancashire hot pot which has been simmering in the slow cooker since early morning.

Rex goes straight into the kitchen to thicken the hot pot. Amela goes into the dining room to set the table. There are only the two of them, she tries hard to lift her flagging spirits. She sets the table with a lace cloth, the gold plated cutlery, and the fine English bone china dinner plates. She finds a bottle of good red wine and pours it into the finest crystal glasses. Rex is almost ready to serve the dinner, this will make them both a bit more cheerful.

The Lancashire hot pot tastes delicious, don't suppose those beer house owners of yesteryear thickened their stews with flavoured gravy browning, come to that, its unlikely they would have lived long enough to be married for fifty years.

Rex cleared the table, Amela sat still, resting her head on her hands, she felt dejected, so unlike her enthusiastic and forward looking self.

What was she going to live for now.? Her friends and ex-pats in France urged them to take up residence there, their eldest son had asked them to come and live in Canada. "I cant do that, I love England too much", Amela said, "I'll visit often but I must have my home in England, I love it here too much" She thought about where she wanted to die. "Bury me on the Pennines " she said, "any place where the windows of my soul could see the beauty of the backbone of England."

Rex too felt dejected. He tried hard to comfort Amela, but with little results. She lifted her head and caught sight of the picture taken fifteen years before. It was of her, seated in front of her three children. Her pretty long haired daughter stood between her tall handsome brothers. The young men were dressed in dark suits and were wearing bow ties, and for all the world could have been the stars in any film or stage show. Amela was wearing a red and black floral dress, her long dark hair swept to one side so clearly showing her still beautiful face.

The Dining Room Wall

The photograph occupies the place of honour on her dining room wall. She remembers the interview for the leprosy job. On her speech about herself she had said, "My life's work, why! my life's work are my three children."

A relation and friend of the family once paid Amela the biggest compliment she'd ever received. "I know three people, the most wonderful people in the world, different in character, all single minded, their aims and ambitions in life unswerving, lives filled with humour and honour, who know where they are going, and its all been your doing Amela"

They no longer needed her, her life's work was finished. She had endeavoured to teach them to be good children, good citizens, and good parents.. What does she do now? Wait with Rex until they are called from above. She rose from the table and walked to the mirror that hung by the picture on the dining room wall. She gazed at her reflection. What did she see? A woman approaching her three score years and ten, her allotted life span. She saw the grey roots of her dyed hair showing through. She saw the spots and lines, the blemishes that pulled the skin of her brown face.

She saw the cataracts that clouded her vision. She thought of her sisters and brothers who all died so young. Steele and Alston had both had bypass operations, themselves knocking on death's door. How can I get away with it much longer.

Strange thing, genes, Alston carried the obvious genes of John William Cranston's family four hundred years after their demise, how could he have resembled someone who had been dead four hundred years?

"The eyes are the windows of the soul", they say. Cataracts cannot cloud the windows of the soul. She looks inwards, her life, her gifts, her marriage, her family, her blessings. She looks back, to her ancestors, their lives, their mistakes, their successes.

She looks around her, the country of her birth India, she is warm and soft hearted towards India. The country of her adoption, she loves England. She loves the countryside, the towns, the cities, the welcome England extends to millions of desperate immigrants, she loves the system, the caring health system, she truly loves England, but most of all she loves the English man she met and married half a century ago

She picked up the birthday card Lizzie had sent her on her nineteenth birthday. It reads - "May God guard and bless you all your days"

"What then can I say to you my children, only this, 'to thine own self be true, it must follow as the night, the day. thou canst not then be false to any man".

The telephone rang.

"Hello Amela, its Jason" that was Gerry's son, he continued, "Just wanted you to be one of the first to know, Samantha has given birth to a beautiful baby boy, we're naming him Gerry".

Amela began to cry, this time with joy, only moments before she was desolate and inward looking, sad because she thought all the good things in life were past. Four of her precious siblings were dead, she thought she was of a generation that was not considered important in the lives of the young, and nobody of her generation mattered. Or so she thought!

She dried her eyes.

"Rex, Rex," she shouted up the stairs. "Listen, I've had an idea, I've had a brilliant idea, come down, I'm going to write a book, you can do the research for me on the internet". She scribbled a list of subjects she wanted Rex to research. It read something like this:-

The British Raj, Famous Anglo Indians, The Hindu caste system, Mahatma Gandhi, The Independence of India , The game of snooker, Indian railways, and Wynberg Allen. I'm going to dedicate it to our children. I'm going to have it published, I'm going to call it THE DINING ROOM WALL.

In conclusion:

I gathered my loved ones around me,
I gazed at each face I adore,
And I heard a voice within me whisper
"This is worth living for."

Printed in Great Britain
by Amazon